Liberalism and Imperial Governance in the Thought of J.S. Mill

Timothy Smith

Liberalism and Imperial Governance in the Thought of J.S. Mill

The Architecture of a Democratization Theorem

VDM Verlag Dr. Müller

Imprint

Bibliographic information by the German National Library: The German National Library lists this publication at the German National Bibliography; detailed bibliographic information is available on the Internet at
http://dnb.d-nb.de.

Any brand names and product names mentioned in this book are subject to trademark, brand or patent protection and are trademarks or registered trademarks of their respective holders. The use of brand names, product names, common names, trade names, product descriptions etc. even without a particular marking in this works is in no way to be construed to mean that such names may be regarded as unrestricted in respect of trademark and brand protection legislation and could thus be used by anyone.

Cover image: www.purestockx.com

Published 2008 Saarbrücken

Publisher:
VDM Verlag Dr. Müller Aktiengesellschaft & Co. KG , Dudweiler Landstr. 125 a,
66123 Saarbrücken, Germany,
Phone +49 681 9100-698, Fax +49 681 9100-988,
Email: info@vdm-verlag.de

Produced in Germany by:
Schaltungsdienst Lange o.H.G., Zehrensdorfer Str. 11, 12277 Berlin, Germany
Books on Demand GmbH, Gutenbergring 53, 22848 Norderstedt, Germany

Impressum

Bibliografische Information der Deutschen Nationalbibliothek: Die Deutsche Nationalbibliothek verzeichnet diese Publikation in der Deutschen Nationalbibliografie; detaillierte bibliografische Daten sind im Internet über http://dnb.d-nb.de abrufbar.

Alle in diesem Buch genannten Marken und Produktnamen unterliegen warenzeichen-, marken- oder patentrechtlichem Schutz bzw. sind Warenzeichen oder eingetragene Warenzeichen der jeweiligen Inhaber. Die Wiedergabe von Marken, Produktnamen, Gebrauchsnamen, Handelsnamen, Warenbezeichnungen u.s.w. in diesem Werk berechtigt auch ohne besondere Kennzeichnung nicht zu der Annahme, dass solche Namen im Sinne der Warenzeichen- und Markenschutzgesetzgebung als frei zu betrachten wären und daher von jedermann benutzt werden dürften.

Coverbild: www.purestockx.com

Erscheinungsjahr: 2008
Erscheinungsort: Saarbrücken

Verlag: VDM Verlag Dr. Müller Aktiengesellschaft & Co. KG , Dudweiler Landstr. 125 a,
D- 66123 Saarbrücken,
Telefon +49 681 9100-698, Telefax +49 681 9100-988,
Email: info@vdm-verlag.de

Herstellung in Deutschland:
Schaltungsdienst Lange o.H.G., Zehrensdorfer Str. 11, D-12277 Berlin
Books on Demand GmbH, Gutenbergring 53, D-22848 Norderstedt

ISBN: 978-3-8364-8309-4

Liberal Imperialism and Imperial Governance in the Thought of J.S. Mill: the architecture of a democratization theorem.

By

Timothy Eric Smith

Table of Contents

Acknowledgements

This work was originally in the form of my M.A. thesis at the University of Victoria and would not have come to fruition if it was not for a number of extraordinary people who have supported me in my scholarly pursuits. First and foremost Professor James Tully has been a superb supervisor and a model scholar. Dr. Tully's scholarship, supervision, and graduate seminars at the University of Victoria are all essential factors in my ability to inquire into the relationship between John Stuart Mill and imperialism and I consider myself extremely fortunate to have had the opportunity to work with him.

Acknowledgement is also due to my excellent committee members, Associate Professor Avigail Eisenberg and Professor Jeremy Webber. A special debt of gratitude is owed to Professor Webber for his wonderfully grueling questions during the defence of this work. I certainly benefited from the experience of facing them. In a similar spirit I would also like to thank Professor Michael Asch for serving as my external examiner.

The University of Victoria which is situated on Coast Salish lands and within indigenous communities, particularly the Songhees and the Saanich First Nations, is an excellent place to study political theory. I have benefited not only from the excellent faculty and fellow graduate students in the Department of Political Science but also from interactions with faculty and graduate students from UVic's Indigenous Governance program and UVic's Law Department. I had the privilege of sharing most of my graduate seminars with amazing students from both Indigenous Governance and Law. I have taken many lessons from sharing ideas and exchanging questions with all of them.

There are also a number of political scientists from the University of British Columbia and the University of British Columbia Okanagan who are very much a part of my completion of this thesis in the roles they played during the four great years of my undergraduate program. Whatever they might make of this work the following people have provided me with extraordinary teaching and support. They are Dr. Barbara Arneil (UBC), Dr. Laura Janara (UBC), Dr. H.B. McCullough (UBCO), and Dr. Mark Warren (UBC). Although not an exhaustive list these individuals had to be mentioned.

I also give thanks to the classmates, friends, and family who read drafts for me. Thanks to Jennifer Chalmers, Norm Olson, Megan Purcell, Chad Reiss, Lyanne Quirt, and Mark Wilson. And a further thanks to my kinship network for their support. These are the Chalmers, Kohlman, Olson, Smith, and Yeo families. I should also give thanks to my niece Equoia for persuading me to put down the books and just play at all the right times.

Introduction

Mill and Imperialism

The *Stanford Encyclopedia of Philosophy's* 2006 portrayal of John Stuart Mill strongly asserts that "we and the world" would "do well to follow Mill" in his ideas.[1] This portrayal of Mill does not comment on nor acknowledge the scholarship produced over the last 12 years that engages with Mill's relationship to imperialism. The *Stanford* portrayal exemplifies the predominant standpoint on Mill and his position in the Western canon in its silence on Mill's relationship to imperialism. Predominant standpoints simply portray Mill as non-problematically striving for the improvement of humankind. But it is a fact that Mill was an innovator and a proponent of imperial theory and practice for the ends of improving humankind along a particular normative axis of civilizational progress. In this thesis I focus on the literature that engages Mill's relationship to imperialism and I hope to reposition Mill more accurately as a thinker whom we and the world would not do well to follow.

The predominant standpoint on Mill aside, over the last 12 years a growing literature has developed that acknowledges Mill's relationship with imperialism.[2] This body of literature encompasses two standpoints on Mill that are alternative to what I have labeled as the predominant standpoint. First there are those who critically explicate aspects of the undeniable relationship between Mill and imperialism, and are what I call critical standpoints. Second there are those who argue that Mill should not be framed as an extensive imperialist or those who argue that Mill's imperial theory is tolerant and just and, therefore, should be turned to for contemporary use; I call these sympathetic standpoints.

Beyond critically explicating these two types of standpoints I more specifically aim to build off this literature and bring to the forefront one very specific part of Mill's relationship to imperialism. I argue that Mill brings together his ideas on imperialism, liberal democracy, and principles of good governance to construct an imperial democratization and good governance theory. In doing so, I show that Mill creates a practical theorem for "civilized" governors to imperially "civilize" and democratize the "non-civilized" for the ends of "civilizational progress" for humankind. Furthermore, I criticize sympathetic standpoints for basing their framing of Mill on an erroneous understanding of Mill's use of the notion of civilization and argue that any call for the application of Mill's imperialism ought to be resisted by those opposed to imperial democratization under the pretense of improving the human condition. Thus this thesis is a critical standpoint primarily intended to explicate Mill's imperial democratization theorem, but is informed by critical literature in a normative posture against the use of Mill's ideas for "the improvement of mankind."

The justifications for the value and significance of carrying out this project have been alluded to but for clarity I will outline them here. First, the predominant standpoint on Mill perpetuates a distorted and incomplete account of Mill's thought by uncritically endorsing his vision while ignoring its core features, imperialism and Mill's civilizational language. Second, Mill has a clear, developed, extensive, and packaged imperial democratization and good governance theorem that he builds and advocates, which to date has not been clearly and completely explicated in scholarship on Mill. Third, whatever the influences and continuities of Millian imperialism are outside of Mill scholarship, phenomena I do not account for in this thesis, within Mill scholarship there are emerging sympathetic standpoints that embrace Millian imperialism as offering guidance to contemporary issues in global politics. I consider it important to identify this emergence and examine these standpoints.

This work is organized into three chapters. The first chapter is a review and assessment of six critical standpoints within the recent secondary literature that is centered on an acknowledgement that there is a significant relationship between Mill and imperialism. I hope to accomplish three broad purposes. First is to outline dimensions of Millian imperialism identified by critical standpoints that I take as important contributions to the reading of Mill I provide in this thesis. Second, I think it is useful to provide an overview of the historical development of the literature that critically acknowledges a connection between Mill and imperialism. Finally, by focusing on the critical standpoints I hope to provide a significant corrective to the distorted portrait of Mill painted by predominant standpoints.

Building off the insights provided by the existing critical standpoints, in the second chapter I focus on Mill's primary texts to explicate his imperial democratization and good governance theorem. Mill's most pertinent works for this purpose are *Considerations on Representative Government* (1861), his article "A Few Words on Non-Intervention" (1859), and his essay "Civilization" (1836). These two first chapters together constitute the first scholarship to frame Mill as an advocate for imperial democratization and identify *Considerations* as his most explicit and extensive treatise on what Mill views as a much needed practical theorem for this purpose.

The third chapter analyzes three recent sympathetic standpoints that have emerged. There are three broad purposes to this chapter. One is to respond to the objections to my critical thesis on Mill that are inherent in this literature. Second is to review and assess this literature as genuine scholarship on Mill and imperialism. And third is to argue against sympathetic literatures that apply and prescribe Millian imperialism to contemporary issues.

Finally, in my conclusion I provide a brief commentary on what this thesis has accomplished and what it has not accomplished in regards to the need for further critical scholarship on Mill and imperialism. Although the main purpose of this thesis is to bring together the literature on Mill and imperialism, and specifically to explicate Mill's imperial democratization and good governance theorem, the normative current that drives this work is most explicit in my posture against the embracing of Mill's imperialism in some of the sympathetic literature.

Before I get to the first chapter I have a brief note on my use of the terms "imperial," "imperialist," and "imperialism." There are many uses and meanings of these terms but by "imperial," "imperialist," and "imperialism" I mean something along the lines of the use that is employed in both the critical and sympathetic literature.[3] I mean the acts, theories, and practices of imposing a particular normative order on others through a mix of intervention and interference. By intervention I mean normative reordering through military force, and by interference I mean normative reordering through character formation *via* cultural, economic, pedagogical, and social and political governance programs.[4]

Chapter 1

Six Critical Standpoints

This chapter's task is to bring together various dimensions of Millian imperialism identified by six critical standpoints within the recent literature on Mill and imperialism. Among the critical standpoints there is a plethora of connected imperial dimensions of Mill that can be abstracted from this literature. I list a variety of these below in an artificially categorical fashion for analytic and communicative clarity.

These dimensions are stated from (A) to (K) in no particular order of significance. (A) Mill's historical and social position in Victorian England as the son of James Mill and employee of the East India Company for 35 years.[5] (B) Mill's relationship to empire and imperialism through the exclusionary and homogenizing logics that extend from the epistemological and ontological bases of Mill's thought, particularly from Mill's liberalism and utilitarianism.[6] (C) The role of Mill's modular notion of maturity in employing and justifying intervention and interference.[7] (D) The civilizational language of "savages" and "barbarians" that is extensively employed by Mill throughout his works and its significance in a comprehensive account of Millian imperialism. (E) The hierarchical typology of forms of governance that corresponds to the hierarchical typology of civilizations.[8] (F) Mill's universal prescription of representative government as the best particular form of government for humanity. (G) Mill's account of the material preconditions and moral preconditions which are required for any nation to be able and willing to acquire and maintain representative government.[9] (H) Mill's prescription of intervention and interference as permissible and obligatory means for mature civilized nations to reorder immature non-civilized nations towards Mill's idealized model of liberal-representative government.[10] (I) Mill's theory employs intervention and interference to internal others as well as external others.[11] (J) Mill's liberal theory of ethology or science of character formation as a form of liberal governmentality and an effort towards perfecting the effectiveness of interference. (K) Millian imperialism operates in the contemporary world.[12]

I do not carry out an account of each of the dimensions in turn. Rather, I select six main critical standpoint authors who have produced scholarship that articulates at least one, and usually many, of these dimensions to varying degrees. I will explicate each author's position and contribution. This review and assessment of each author in chronological order will, when read together, encompass an account of these related dimensions. By outlining the authors in chronological order I hope to provide a sense of how a growing recognition and criticism of Millian imperialism occurred between 1994 and 2005.

Bhikhu Parekh: Superior Peoples and the Narrowness of Mill's Liberalism

Bhikhu Parekh was one of the first authors to substantially engage and initiate a critical reframing of Mill with an acknowledgement of the significance of imperialism.[13] Parekh argues that Millian liberalism is penetrated to its core by the 19th-century experience of British colonialism and imperialism, as this experience shaped Millian liberalism's self-definition.[14] He writes that during the 19th century, liberalism most extensively and influentially through John Stuart Mill became "missionary, ethnocentric, and narrow, dismissing non-liberal ways of life and thought" as "primitive" and in material and moral need of the "liberal civilizing mission."[15] Moreover, Parekh sees the contemporary world entangled with Millian liberalism in that today's liberals have not yet fully liberated themselves from this Millian legacy.[16]

Parekh explicates that for Mill "man was a progressive being" whose "ultimate destiny" was to "secure the fullest development of his intellectual, moral, aesthetic and other faculties".[17] Here Parekh's interpretation of Mill is largely correct in that it highlights Mill's normative project to have humanity progress towards the "best thing" it can "possibly become" along the particularly Millian understanding of intellectual, moral, and aesthetic development.[18] That said, I will provide a partial corrective to the emphasis in Parekh's rendering of progress as "ultimate destiny" in a moment.

To understand Parekh's perspective it is necessary to understand that Parekh frames Mill's thought as fundamentally distinguishing superior peoples and inferior peoples. This is Parekh's account of what I call Mill's civilizational language. Parekh illustrates how Mill "divided societies into two," the civilized and non-civilized, the European and the other, or the superior and the inferior.[19] Parekh elucidates that for Mill the civilized "tended to do" what "they ought to do" according to Mill's normative vision. In other words the civilized were able and willing to do what liberal ways required of them to progress towards the best that humanity could possibly be. For Mill, Victorian England of his day was the closest realization to this ideal in the modern world.[20]

The non-civilized, on the other hand, "had to be educated into the civilized normative order and, until such time as they were ready, held in check."[21] Parekh is correct on this point, for Mill the "non-civilized" means, for example, "North American Indians" whom he categorizes as "savages" who are not yet ready for pedagogical guidance and therefore require to be enslaved by force. Enslavement constitutes a double move in Mill to hold "savages" in check as well as a first step to getting the "savage" ready for forthcoming modes of interference.[22] The non-civilized also refers to "barbarians" of "Hindustan" who were more advanced and ready for pedagogical imperialism than "savages." Note here how the civilizational language in Mill's thought operates in two ways. One as a binary between the civilized and non-civilized and second as a linear continuum running from the bottom rung of savage to the top rung of civilized. The two forms provide Millian imperialism the governmental flexibility to frame others as existing between two hierarchical categories such as semi-civilized (between barbarian and civilized on the Millian continuum) or simply as the binary other. The advantage of this for Millian imperial governance is that for any one particular "barbarian" nation it provides two sets of arguments with two different results. One source justifies interference (experiments in self-government within the empire based on the more sophisticated continuum form) or a justification for intervention (despotic enforcement of order and the exclusion from self-government for a dependency based on the binary form).

One of the strengths of Parekh's work is that he emphasizes Mill's civilizational typology as not only constituting abstract theoretical concepts but as live judgments by live people towards other living peoples in a lived colonial and imperial context. Furthermore, Parekh encapsulates the connotative spirit of Mill's civilizational language as a dimension of Millian imperialism effectively dividing the world into superior peoples and inferior peoples, and thereby justifying the imperial intervention and interference of the latter by the former. But Parekh's work does not detail the two different operative forms that the civilizational language takes in Mill's thought: the binary form and the continuum form. Nor does Parekh detail the way these forms of civilizational language signify corresponding forms of government. That said, the binary form of the civilizational language is basically identified by Parekh's phraseology of superior peoples and inferior peoples.

Another important feature of Parekh's phraseology is that it articulates how it is that even if Mill rejected the biological racist theories of his contemporaries he nevertheless justifies violent normative reordering and hierarchies based on ethnocentrically based judgments on others and difference.[23] It is worth noting that if Mill had brought the premise of biological racism into his project of normatively reordering others, then the project itself would have become logically perplexed. This is because Mill's project—to have superior peoples, especially the British, reorder inferior peoples such as the "barbarians" of "Hindustan" through coercion and violence—relies on the premise that inferiors can and often should be civilized.[24] Mill's civilizing premise and the premise of biological racism, although coexisting in imperial practices, are not logically commensurable. Mill's extensive ethnocentrism and his civilizing premise logically go together in Mill's thought.

Parekh also connects Mill's civilizational language to the concept of maturity when he notes that those whom Mill calls "civilized" are those human beings who have, in Mill's words, attained the requisite "maturity of their faculties" to allow the capacity of being guided to their own improvement by conviction or persuasion."[25] This connection becomes important to my reading of Mill for three reasons. One is that the distinction between "civilized" and "non-civilized" is often analogous to the distinction between the "mature" and the "immature." Second, as I will elaborate in my explication of Eddy Souffrant's critical standpoint below, the notion of maturity operates in both Mill's "domestic" philosophy of reordering internal immature barbarians and in his "philosophy of international affairs" of reordering external barbarians.[26] Third, maturity and the method of maturation is a field of great concern to Mill as emphasized in his theory of ethology or the science of character formation. Mill's ethology is treated in more detail in my explication of Jennifer Pitts' and Melanie White's critical standpoints below.[27]

It is important to correct Parekh's perspective as outlined above by noting that Mill did not see "progress" as humanity's "ultimate destiny" but as an ontological normative goal towards which humanity should consciously drive itself.[28] The insecurity over the non-inevitability of Mill's particular ideology of progress, as Parekh notes, is partially what motivates Mill's willingness to endorse coercion and violence to enforce progress on those unfit (unable and unwilling) to develop.[29] This is partly why it is usually permissible and often obligatory for superior peoples to employ intervention and imperial interference against inferior peoples, because "progress" is not natural in relation to inferior peoples' constitution. Therefore, a great portion of humanity for Mill in fact all non-Europeans of Mill's day is seen as incapable and unwilling to move towards this progress. In this way, the non-civilized pose a great threat, through their difference, to all of humanity.[30]

Parekh also recognizes that although Mill took the concept and process of progress for granted in normative terms, Mill does not do so in descriptive terms. Parekh notes this when he argues that Mill was "not really concerned with the East" but "constructed the East" with two objectives in mind.[31] Note here that Mill takes a spatial-temporal framework for granted in which there are only three possibilities for historical movement: regress, stillness, and progress.[32] The first objective is to show the British "what would happen if they did not cultivate the spirit of individuality" and the second is to argue that other nations who did not have this spirit "needed external help" and therefore the British and its selected allies were justified in employing intervention and interference to this end.[33]

This brings me to Parekh's final point. Parekh flags the role that Mill's narrow and limited conception of diversity plays in Millian imperialism. Parekh's important contribution here is his identification of the fact that Millian liberalism values "not diversity *per se* but *liberal* diversity" which in Mill's thought is "confined within the narrow limits" of his "model of human excellence" which is entwined with the civilizational language, the concept of maturity, and the normative project of reordering inferior peoples through coercion and violence.[34] Part of Mill's story of why Europeans are civilized and non-Europeans are not is that Europeans have had a history of liberal diversity whereas the stagnant and stationary existence of non-Europeans has not and therefore non-Europeans have been unable to consciously progress.[35] This is an important critical point on Mill especially in light of some contemporary scholarship that uses the language of diversity in Mill's thought as evidence to the fact that it is inappropriate to read Mill as an imperialist or as an unjust imperialist.[36]

Uday Singh Mehta : J.S. Mill and the Homogenization of Unfamiliar Difference

A second critical standpoint is provided by Uday Singh Mehta in his 1999 book *Liberalism and Empire: A Study in Nineteenth Century Liberal Thought.*[37] Through the case of British rule of India, Mehta examines the relationship between British political thinkers and the justification for British Empire. Mehta finds that the liberal political thinkers, particularly John Stuart Mill, were essential in providing a justification for

British Empire.[38] Mehta explicates and accounts for the way in which Mill's justification of empire entails a number of related dimensions, each working to justify imperialism. These include: economic, epistemological, ethical, historical, juridical, ontological pedagogical, political, social, and temporal dimensions.[39]

For Mehta, what brings these different dimensions together into a coherent and pervasive justification for empire is the fusing of three major aspects of Mill's thought: (1) ideals of progress, civilization, and historical development,[40] what I term the civilizational language and what Parekh frames as the division of the world into superior and inferior peoples; (2) a reformed political liberalism;[41] (3) and the utilitarianism J.S. Mill had inherited and modified from Jeremy Bentham and his father James Mill, which the younger Mill used to fundamentally transform political liberalism.[42]

Roughly, not exclusively, the first major aspect (the civilizational language) works to bring the historical, the temporal, and the ontological into J.S. Mill's thought. The second major aspect (Mill's reformed political liberalism) works to bring the economic, the epistemological, and the political into Mill's thought. The third major aspect (modified utilitarianism) works to bring the ethical, the social, and the juridical into Mill's thought. The pedagogical dimension of JS Mill's justification for British empire seems to be strongly reinforced by all three of these aspects of his thought but originates in the proto-liberalism of John Locke.[43]

Mehta moves towards connecting his in-depth account of Millian imperialism to Mill's imperial democratization and good governance theory when he outlines Mill's pedagogical imperialism. Mehta explains that J.S. Mill's view of the British as forming a "government of leading strings," as a means of "gradually training the people to walk as one" constitutes a trope in imperial discourse because

> They all coalesce around the same general point: India is a child for which the empire offers the prospect of legitimate and progressive parentage and toward which Britain, as a parent, is similarly obliged and competent ....The idea has a distinguished pedigree and in the liberal tradition originates in Locke's characterization of tutelage as a necessary stage through which children must be trained before they acquire the reason requisite for expressing contractual consent[44]

Mill's translation of liberal pedagogical imperialism into a democratization program through his "government of leading strings," which is analyzed by Mehta above, is a core aspect of Mill's imperial democratization and good governance theorem.

Ultimately, Mehta views Mill's political thought as attempting to reconcile the seemingly irreconcilable, that is, the modern enlightenment language of humanity with the violent inhumanity of the modern British Empire. In doing so Mehta illustrates why it is that the two phenomena go together, because one phenomenon is not well understood in a coherent fashion without the other. Therefore the tensions that some see in Mill's enlightenment project of establishing and defending his particular principles of freedom, liberty and Mill's justification of British empire and imperialism are reconciled. They are reconciled into a coherent system of thought in that the enlightenment aspects, Mill's liberalism and utilitarianism, provide the epistemological and ontological premises of Mill's imperialism. Hence Mill's enlightenment humanism is inextricably linked to his imperialism because these fundamental premises require the homogenization of any unfamiliar difference they encounter in the world.[45] In other words, Mill is using imperialism as a means to pursue his humanist goals.

Eddy Souffrant: Maturity and the No Harm Principle in Mill's Imperialism

A third critical standpoint is provided by Eddy Souffrant, in his 2000 book *Formal Transgression: John Stuart Mill's Philosophy of International Affairs*. Souffrant delineates a philosophy of international affairs from Mill's work to show that one "would be warranted to claim that Mill's attempted justification of colonization was in effect an advocacy of imperialism," an advocacy that has relevance and continuity in contemporary imperial practice of the post-colonial era.[46] Souffrant provides an important interpretation of the roles that the notions of individuality, conformity, and maturity play in Mill's political theory and in his advocacy of imperialism.[47] Here Souffrant provides an account of the how the mature become the guardians of Mill's normative order, using intervention and interference to protect and impose proper ways of being both domestically against internal "barbarians" and internationally against external "barbarians."[48] We should recall from Parekh's work that the language of maturity in Mill's thought operates at times as a synonym for the civilizational language. Souffrant's contribution is a unique and I think correct commentary on the function of a modular notion of maturity employed by Mill, which Souffrant uses to outline the continuity between Mill's domestic political theory and his philosophy of international affairs.

Relying on chapters 3 and 4 of *On Liberty*, with an eye towards Mill's philosophy of international affairs, Souffrant illustrates that Mill's "conception of individuality is a restricted one" that depends on his concept of maturity and "permits interference with an individual whose individuality is thought to deviate from that conception of maturity."[49] Souffrant notes that in *On Liberty* when Mill speaks of individuality, he is referring to an attribute of mature individuals, human beings who have been brought up within the confines of particular societies. Mature individuals enjoy having had a formative period contributing to their maturity. The individuality expressed by mature individuals presupposes thus a social training.[50]

According to Souffrant, Mill prescribes that the intellectual part of humanity ought to socially engineer the correct formative training to liberate the rest of humanity from custom and tradition.[51] This insight by Souffrant illustrates why, in Mill's thought, the mature people of a nation ought to interfere and intervene with the immature, and, likewise, at the international level, the "mature" civilized nations ought to interfere and intervene with "immature," "backward" nations.[52] Hence, Souffrant is able to see the continuity between Mill's domestic political theory and his philosophy of international affairs which justifies colonialism and advocates imperialism.

There are two key passages from Souffrant's work that give insight on the role of maturity in Millian imperialism. First Souffrant writes that:

> The two sides of Mill's theory are on the one hand that society has had its time to mold the individual and is in need of no additional resources to control the individual, and on the other that the individual should not be interfered with once individuality has been reached unless she causes harm to another. Mill's theory thus suggests that interference before the period of maturity (however vaguely construed) is justified if not required. This interference denies or considers irrelevant the will of the so-called immature. For Mill, the interaction between the individual and society is such that when one speaks of individuality one is referring to the attribute of a mature, rational, thinking individual full of age. Only when those attributes are assigned can that individual be entitled to the freedoms of individuality. At that point the requirements of non-interference apply and the individual becomes eligible to receive the kinds of protection Mill believes is due her society in large.[53]

This passage by Souffrant locates Mill's no-harm principle" in a way that helps the contemporary theorist to discern it as a principle that polices people, wherever they are situated in a binary of mature and immature or on a continuum from mature to immature. This is because the immature are excluded from the outset from Mill's modular form of maturity[54] and therefore are excluded from the protection of the no harm principle. Mature people, on the other hand, are included in Mill's modular form of maturity only by virtue of their conformity to this module through social training.[55] For the mature, this protection is terminated if the mature deviate from the space of maturity through barbaric or immature conduct.[56]

Souffrant's contribution regarding the role of maturity and the no-harm principle in the context of intervention and interference is significant to my reading of Mill. It is significant especially when combined with Mill's view that the immature and the uncivilized, through their conduct and the fact of their very existence, cause harm to humanity in general, and therefore require intervention and interference for protective and reordering purposes. By bringing these points together, we can discern how and why Mill's modular notion enables the mature community to intervene and interfere with those without recognized mature status, because for Mill people labeled immature, deviant, and barbarian harm humanity by the fact of their existence and alternative practices of being. Ultimately the no-harm principle based on Mill's modular form of maturity imperially polices both the mature and the immature—the latter through initial and perpetual exclusion until such time as they are reordered and become mature; the former through their very inclusion coupled with the threat of expulsion from this status-group by their peer-community constituted by the mature/s. Taken as such, Souffrant's contribution indicates how the no-harm principle in the context of its preconditions is useful as a technique and a tactic to progress towards (or construct) the universal normative order Mill idealizes and prescribes.

The second key passage in Souffrant further elucidates how the role of maturity functions in Mill's thought *via* the interaction between society and the individual:

> there is an imposition on the individual during his interaction with society. The vagueness of the term maturity and the fact that the immature human being is the less powerful in the interaction means that he ultimately suffers in the exchange. *By the time the individual is considered to have reached the level of maturity that theoretically protects him from the interference of outsiders, he has already been coerced to conform to a societal conception of individuality.*[57]

This constructivist power dynamic identified by Souffrant portrays one way in which Mill hopes to achieve the social training of individuals to create and protect a particular way of being. This dynamic, however, also applies to the interaction between a society of "mature" nations, known today as the international community,[58] and individual nations outside of this community.[59]

In sum, Souffrant shows that the concept of maturity is significant in Mill's thought for three related and overlapping reasons: (1) it is a mechanism by which the subjects and agents of interference and intervention are identified; the mature agent can and often should intervene and interfere with the immature subject; (2) those people considered mature and free from intervention now were once correctly intervened with as children along their development towards maturity, ensuring that they fit Mill's modular form of individuality and maturity; (3) and the mature are also policed through the no-harm principle in that if they deviate from its conditions they become subject to the sanctions of intervention.

Jennifer Pitts: The Civilizational Language and the Pax Britannica

A fourth critical standpoint is provided by Jennifer Pitts in her 2005 work "James and John Stuart Mill: The Development of Imperial Liberalism in Britain."[60] Pitts argues that of all the modern thinkers privileged in the Western canon, it is the two Mills who most extensively justify and advocate colonialism and imperialism based on a philosophy of history which at its core rested on their civilizational language of inferior and superior peoples.[61] Pitts is concerned with contrasting the two Mills with other canonical thinkers of the modern era to argue that figures such as Adam Smith, Edmund Burke, and Jeremy Bentham are anti-imperialists who at the very least do not participate in the extensive imperial dimensions that one finds "most forcefully" in the thought of J.S. Mill.[62] Pitts is particularly interested in distinguishing between Scottish Enlightenment social development theories which she argues had a "complex gradation of four or more stages" through which Scottish historians "could discuss degrees of complexity among various settled societies" without necessarily hierarchically privileging one culture over others as superior.[63] I agree with Pitts that among modern canonical thinkers J.S. Mill has most forcefully advocated imperialism with superior peoples governing others on the justification that it is for the benefit of "others" and the benefit of humanity. I, however, do not agree with Pitts' representations of many other earlier Western thinkers and the Western tradition in general as anti-imperialist. Nor do I think a four-stage rubric for examining cultures is particularly complex and normatively beneficial or neutral, but this is beyond the scope of my thesis.

Pitts begins by providing an account of James Mill's imperialism and its relevance to J.S. Mill, especially in terms of the philosophy of history they share (it should be noted that the younger Mill, as Pitts outlines, provides a more thoroughly theorized and forceful version of this philosophy of history).[64] Pitts situates the elder Mill as "somewhere between the theories of social development central to the Scottish Enlightenment and the theory of progress distinctive of J.S. Mill's liberalism."[65] She notes that James Mill's highly regarded and influential work *The History of British India* (first published in 1817), and other articles by James Mill, argued that it was "Britain's duty as a civilized and progressive nation to impose its rule on India" for the sake of Britain's Indian subjects.[66] Pitts also notes how James Mill's radical criticism of the British government in domestic affairs coexisted with his belief in the "superiority of British politics and culture."[67] Pitts adds that in addition to "believing that utility could be adopted" as a "standard of judgment for any society" James Mill claimed that Britain ranked highest among all nations and that its laws "ought to be imposed on backward nations."[68] Pitts also notes how James Mill proposed the "quite extraordinary solution of having a member of the British royal family sent out to found a hereditary emperorship of Hindustan, to govern with the help of British advisers, and to encourage settlement by 'Europeans of all descriptions.'"[69]

Her work also frames the relationship between James Mill and John Stuart Mill in terms that move towards the spirit of my reading of J.S. Mill as an imperial democratization and good governance theorist. Pitts writes that James Mill utilizes his philosophy of history to develop an imperial theory of governance, writing that James Mill adopted a "standard of utility" with "an idea of progressive social development" from Scottish Enlightenment thinkers.[70] This resulted in a "problematic fusion" and an "index of progress in which utility is the sole standard against which any nation can be measured" in a civilizational binary or along a civilizational scale.[71] Pitts connects this to a good governance theory when she writes that James Mill seems to have seen his project as the application of philosophical history to good government: the technique of conjectural history should not be simply a matter of theoretical reflection but a tool of utilitarian governance.[72]

Pitts' account of James Mill illustrates, as we know from Mehta's work, that there are "echoes" of James Mill in the younger Mill's "advocacy of progressive despotism."[73] Although JS Mill argued for imperial governance through the East India Company and James Mill for the installation of a member of the royal family to consolidate direct British rule of India, Pitts reminds us that whatever their differences both Mills argued "that the British empire could be justified not only by domestic improvements but also by the pax Britannica it would create."[74]

Pitts also discusses the role of individual and national character formation in Millian imperialism. Pitts writes it "was the younger Mill's efforts to introduce into utilitarian thought a consideration of character, both individual and national, and his belief in progress which he saw as an essential element of liberty that mark" JS Mill's imperialism.[75]

In relation to these contributions, Pitts also provides valuable points on JS Mill's "meaning of nationality," the relationship between material and moral development in his imperial thought, and his narrow concept of diversity. She also argues against the simple position that the now politically incorrect and objectionable civilizational language employed by JS Mill in his historical context was merely the result of a human being working through the natural language of his times.[76] With the exception of the last point, I touch on each of these to close off my discussion of Pitt's work.

Pitts writes that JS Mill used nationality as a normative category and as a descriptive term. In the normative sense "nationality was an achievement of civilization" bringing with it recognition and rights in the "international sphere."[77] What Pitts does not add is that a similar logic applies for Mill at the intra-national level. Becoming a member of the community is the achievement of the individual entering society as a responsible member with the capacity to responsibly self-govern, thereby gaining recognition and rights in the "social sphere" such as the protection and privilege of the no harm principle.[78] The descriptive sense of the term refers to people who have modernized in an economic sense, having the economic systems and commercial development along the lines of what existed in Britain and Europe generally. This understanding by Pitts is important as it maps onto JS Mill's two meanings of civilization, one which has a broad normative meaning and one which is a descriptive term, there is always an element of the descriptive term when Mill wields his notion of civilization. Both of these two meanings correspond to and crystallize with Mill's distinction between material development and moral development and the relationship between the two. This relationship is noted by Pitts when she writes that in JS Mill's support of Auguste Comte's view of history:

> Mill offered one of his most complex accounts of social development, recognizing stages of intellectual development, the effects of the division of labor on social evolution, and the interaction between material and intellectual causes in the progress of society.[79]

Pitts' account of diversity is along the lines provided by Parekh and Souffrant but is worth explicating because it is expressed a little bit differently. Parekh asserted that Mill's concept of diversity is a narrow concept within the confines of his liberal and progressive ideals. Souffrant illustrates how Mill's diversity is a concept narrowed by the confines of Mill's modular conception of mature or maturity and individuality. Pitts accounts for Mill's narrow concept of diversity in two passages. First, Pitts writes:

Although Mill regularly cautioned that nations and national characters must be understood as diverse, as formed by 'time and place, and circumstance,' he nonetheless tended at just these moments to reduce diversity among societies to variation along a single axis of progress. Mill's perfectionism, his belief in the self-development as a preeminent moral duty and his conviction that societies, like individuals, must continue to 'improve' or else stagnate or decline, supported a view of social progress that in many of its details restated and affirmed the much less complex ideas of his father....Mill takes national differences to signify degrees of advancement in a rigid hierarchy of progress; and, like his father, he characterizes members of "backward" societies as children.[80]

This is clear enough and brings together the relationship between Mill's modular concept of maturity, Mill's civilizational language, and Mill's narrow concept of diversity. The second key passage from Pitts is her analysis of Mill's critique of Bentham that he failed to recognize political institutions "in a higher light" as the "principal means of the social education of people" and therefore lacked the knowledge that "the same institutions will no more suit two nations in different stages of civilization, than the same lessons will suit children of different ages."[81] Contingent examples of these differences, for Mill, are "North American Indians" who as "savages" require "taming" versus "Asiatics" as "barbarians" who require hardening."[82] Here Pitts gestures towards a cultural moral spectrum in Mill that is more clearly outlined in the discussion of Beate Jahn's work below.[83]

The notion that Mill has a narrow conception of diversity is largely shared among the critical standpoint theorists including Parekh, Methta, Pitts, and Beate Jahn. The point that needs to be noted for my purposes is that for Mill, if diverse ways of being do not move people to progress towards his particular ideal of civilization and representative government, therefore satisfying the moral and material preconditions required for this achievement, then this diversity is intolerable and open to normative reordering through intervention and interference which is the *sine quo non* of imperialism generally. As we will see in turning to Beate Jahn below, the material and moral preconditions by definition exclude the possibility for deep plurality and extensive multiplicity of diverse ways of being in the ideal Millian world.

Beate Jahn: Mill's Civilizational Language and Appropriate Forms of Government

A fifth critical standpoint is provided in Beate Jahn's 2005 article "Barbarian thoughts: imperialism in the philosophy of John Stuart Mill." Jahn's article is the scholarship on Mill that most closely intersects and overlaps with my critical standpoint on Mill. Jahn begins by noting how predominant standpoints have recently come "under critical scrutiny" as authors such as Mehta, Parekh, and Souffrant have argued that Mill's liberalism is "inextricably linked to imperialism, which, in turn, is reproduced through liberal practices in the contemporary world."[84] Jahn argues that the disciplinary separation between international relations (IR) and political theory has "led in both disciplines to an unreflected perpetuation of Mill's philosophy of history" upon which Mill's imperialism and its perpetuation in contemporary liberal international theories rests.[85]

To deliver this thesis Jahn reconstructs Mill's philosophy of history,[86] Mill's theory of international relations,[87] and Mill's political theory[88] and then connects each through Mill's imperialism because the latter two components of Mill's thought are necessarily contingent on his philosophy of history that is "rooted in a need to justify the political inequality of humanity on cultural grounds."[89] At certain points Jahn's account of Mill's philosophy of history moves more towards connecting Mill's civilizational language to what I frame as Mill's imperial democratization and good governance theory.

Jahn's move towards the critical standpoint I take is contained the passage below:

> Mill's philosophy of history, then, contains the four broad stages of civilisational development—savagism, slavery, barbarism and civilisation—and he identifies the force which drives this development, *namely the mode of government*. Since development along civilisational lines is not automatic, and since stagnation entails the grave danger of conquest and backward development, human beings have to strive for the next level of development by *establishing the appropriate form of government* for this purpose. This philosophy of history is the basis of Mill's theory of international relations.[90]

The last words above could as easily and more aptly have read "...the basis of Mill's imperial theory of democratization and good governance."[91] This is indicative of the fact that Jahn's critical standpoint that "Mill developed a distinctive theory of international relations on the basis of his philosophy of history" is commensurable to my standpoint and offers some valuable building blocks for my identification of Mill's imperial democratization and good governance theorem outlined in the next chapter..

For example, as shown above Jahn explicates her understanding of Mill's civilizational language as the fundamental premise by which Mill consciously strives towards his normative ideal and reorders others towards his particular conception of civilization through intervention and interference.[92] In this Jahn moves even further towards my critical standpoint when she notes that for Mill civilization and therefore representative government require "certain kinds of preconditions."[93]

Jahn even goes some distance towards outlining how Millian imperialism resembles the core of contemporary democratization and good governance theories in that Jahn briefly mentions democratization thinker Samuel Huntington as well as notable liberal theorists such as Francis Fukuyama as intellectuals that promote contemporary imperial projects which rest on Mill's hierarchical civilizational division of the world as the basis upon which peoples are subject to intervention and interference by those at the top of the hierarchy.[94] Jahn explicitly agrees with the critical standpoint that Mill's "justification of colonialism is of continuing relevance today," as Eddy Souffrant has argued, because it provides the basis for the "implementation of a foreign policy of intervention" which "constitutes the fundamental nature of imperialism."[95]

Given the importance of Jahn's identification of Mill's material and moral preconditions that are required of civilization and representative government it is worth outlining Jahn's account of them here. Material preconditions means modernization such as the building of infrastructure, "in particular roads" as well as the development of a commercial market economy. Jahn spends little time on the material preconditions asserting that "generally Mill is much more interested in what he calls the moral preconditions for civilization and representative government."[96]

Even with this brief treatment one can see, as I do, that the material preconditions map onto contemporary democratization theory which theorizes how development and liberalization ought to be instituted in illiberal non-democratic orders in the world—with some arguing material development is a precondition to democracy and good governance (the liberalization first thesis) and some arguing that the material and moral preconditions need to be instantiated simultaneously in illiberal contexts because the two are mutually necessary to each other (the simultaneous conditions thesis).[97] Mill's imperial democratization and good governance theory provides premises for both of these types of democratization and good governance approaches. The substance of contemporary democratization theories are beyond the scope of this thesis.

Mill is not only quite concerned with the material preconditions, *contra* Jahn, but is extensively concerned with how such conditions relate to the moral preconditions and *vice versa*. Both the material and the moral preconditions, including the relationship between the material and the moral state and condition of particular peoples, are integral to Mill's broader civilizational project of cultural and political normative reordering. Mill's moral preconditions are explained by Jahn in the passage below:

> If a people is very passive they will not fight for their freedom when attacked and would choose tyrants as their representatives. And only despotic rule or a general massacre could have emancipated the serfs of Russia. If a people is ignorant and lacks mental cultivation, if it is gullible, it may be cheated out of its freedom. If a people is too rude to control its passions, to forgo private conflict, too proud not to avenge wrongs done to them directly, it is not ready for self-government. The existences of prejudices, adherence to old habits and a general incapacity to adapt to and accept constant changes are hindrances to self-government; and, generally, not clearly specified 'positive defects of national character'.[98]

Jahn's explication here illustrates that there is a proper moral middle ground for Mill between people who are too rude to effectively control (such as "North American Indians" Mill frames as "savages") and people who are too passive to actively and consciously ensure the continuation of civilization (such as the "Hindoos" of "Hindustan" Mill frames as "barbarians"). Jahn articulates the importance of this middle ground and the moral preconditions generally to Mill's imperial democratization and good governance theorem when she writes that for Mill "[c]ivilizational development is therefore not to be expected as a matter of course but must be pursued consciously" and the "most potent means" of "preparing people for the next stage of civilizational development" is "the form of government."[99]

Jahn completes the account noting that whether a people are "savages" or "barbarians", at the extreme of rudeness or the extreme of passivity, for Mill there are only two ways a people can move towards progress and civilization: the rare exception of government "through an indigenous leader of extraordinary genius" or "government through a culturally superior power carrying the people 'rapidly through several stages of progress'".[100] Mill prescribes the latter because he thinks it is the only practical of the two since an able and willing indigenous leader is "rare".[101] Mill's interest in employing multiple strategies to standardize conduct across populations through character formation congruent with liberal sensibilities thereby promoting civilizational progress is outlined in Melanie White's work which I discuss below.

Melanie White: Mill's Imperialism and the Science of Character Formation

Thus far, the outline of the five authors above enunciates a number of the related dimensions of Millian imperialism as a normative project to reorder the others of the world through intervention and interference which is contingent on, and necessarily connected to, Mill's civilizational language. Yet if the portrait that this ensemble of critical literature paints is correct, would Mill not have attempted an elaborate theory for this purpose? After all if Mill's liberal imperialism aims to reorder alternative ways of being in the world by molding internal and external "barbarians" through means of interference and intervention to form and reform the character of "others", as an empiricist would Mill not have been interested in the details of how to form character in practice through modes of interference? The answer is that Mill did indeed attempt such a theory. In his work *System of Logic*, Mill articulates a theory of ethology as a science of character formation and Melanie White contributes an examination of this in relation to Mill's imperialism and civilizational language, which I turn to now.[102]

Melanie White's 2005 article "The liberal character of ethological governance" uses Foucauldian inspired governmentality theory to explicate ways in which Mill's ethology is a theory of liberal ethological governance. [103] In doing so, White provides an account of Mill's ethology in an effort to "shed some light" on the "apparent rekindling of interest in character and its formation" and Mill's "rehabilitation in the twentieth century" as a "*liberal* philosopher *par excellence*" in the contemporary world.[104] Hence one can see her work as delineating some of the continuities of Millian imperialism from the 19th century into the contemporary world, at least the conception of imperialism as normative reordering imposed through intervention and interference that frames this thesis.

By "ethological governance" White means "the set of practices that is organized by a developmental notion of human conduct (i.e. character) that operates as a standard of liberal government and serves as an index for the responsible exercise of freedom."[105] For White ethological governance "establishes a context that harnesses character as a tool for social and political transformation" and the liberal ethological governance that Mill's theory articulates theorizes some of the "various ways" liberal ethological governance "individualizes personal character through disciplined self-governance and totalizes it by standardizing conduct across populations".[106]

White sees these theoretical points at play historically, loosely "based on the work of John Stuart Mill,"[107] in the popular practices of government in Britain and North America during the late 19th and early 20th centuries.[108] White identifies how the notion of "character operates" within Mill's liberal ethological governance "as the principal point of contact between technologies of the self and technologies of power, and helps to structure the possible action of oneself and others."[109] White writes that in "governing through agents and not acts, ethological governance adopts character as a general way of conceptualizing human conduct."[110] More specifically, White elaborates that there are particular standards of character that are set up as the "principal criterion for evaluating the successful individuation of the liberal subject."[111] These would include the notions of civility, individuality, liberty, progress, maturity, and self-control as the main ideals that underwrite Mill's thought as seen through the critical standpoints discussed above.

White provides an account of the "critical channels" of Millian-type liberal ethological governance throughout the 19th and 20th century which I think provides a simplified but accurate portrayal of Mill's science of character formation. The typical channels involve the moral education of children through particular forms of family, school, and community clubs (such as Boy Scouts and Girl Guides) as sites of character formation. White highlights some of the successful techniques of character formation, for example the discipline and regime of learning the details of grammar and memorizing the morals of fables.[112] For White these sites and techniques of character formation in ethological governance are institutes to ensure "the responsible practice of freedom."[113] The difference between good governance and bad governance is making sure there is not too much governance or too little governance in their effects on character based on the environmental conditions and capacities of the governed or in ideal conditions the self-governing subjects.[114]

In explicating Mill's ethology White notes that "Mill's interest to develop a "science of character formation" is easily situated in the context of his other writings that use character as a means for political reform"[115] but more extensively as a means of normative reordering through intervention and interference. This is reflected in White's work when she writes:

> Mill intended his version of ethology to be a science that would examine how circumstances mould and shape individuals, nations and races....He hoped that in his hands ethology could be used to identify those particular social conditions that were constitutive of the dispositions of specific character types. It would ultimately serve as a normative project that could offer insights into the conditions of possibility for the development of a form of character appropriate for liberal sensibilities.[116]

To elaborate, take two examples in Mill's thought. For Mill "savages" require force to enslave their societies (in this case the most extensive governance and control imaginable is the appropriate amount of governance for character formation).[117] In contrast the mature country of Britain is so civilized that even strong democratically formulated and self-imposed policies might be too much governance that would infringe on the privacy and genius of the best while eroding and homogenizing the very diverse[118], in Mill's narrow liberal sense of diverse, character that ensures that freedom is practiced responsibly and progress is pursued consciously. Here governing very little is the appropriate level of governance.

The Millian dimensions of imperialism such as the civilizational language and the concept of maturity intersect and are congruent with White's account of Mill's ethological governance as seen when she writes that the:

> developmental view of human conduct fosters a paternalism that targets subjects that ostensibly need 'improvement', such as the poor, indigenous peoples, children, and colonial others. Here ethological governance operates under the guise of 'reform' or 'philanthropic' projects that are typically based on progressivist or civilizational narratives. Character comes to operate as a liberal norm that carves out exceptions in order to deny individuals or groups certain rights until they are capable of demonstrating effective self-government. Consequently, the right to demand rights by individuals and groups who are

governed ethologically has typically required the demonstration of character through effective self-discipline and self-control before they display sufficient character in order to be 'free.'[119]

The role of these channels and techniques of ethological governance in 19th century imperialism, and their continuity into the contemporary world are captured by Edward Said's third chapter of *Culture and Imperialism* titled "Resistance and Opposition". Said writes:

> Imperialism after all was a cooperative venture, and a salient trait of its modern form is that it was (or claimed to be) an educational movement; it set out quite consciously to modernize, develop, instruct and civilize. The annals of schools, missions, universities, scholarly societies, hospitals in Asia, Africa, Latin America, Europe, and America are filled with this history, which over time established so called modernizing trends as much as it muted the harsher aspects of imperialist domination. But at its center it preserved the 19th century divide between native and Westerner.[120]

Note here how Said's work captures the relationship between these channels of ethological governance and the civilizational language. This passage does not capture, however, the intensity, extensiveness, and sophistication of ethological channels and techniques of liberal governance as a science of character formation. The latter is White's contribution.

In sum, White's article makes a critical contribution to understanding Millian imperialism in two primary ways. First, Mill's ethology is linked to Mill's normative project of reordering the others of the world "towards liberal sensibilities" through a form of ethology with its "specific focus on the ethical dimensions of [liberal and progressive] *character* formation."[121] Second, it is linked to Mill's civilizational language, ideology of progress, and pedagogical imperialism in general, all of which are shown to be intrinsic to Mill's normative project which as a form of governance theory has continued to operate into the contemporary world.[122]

The six standpoints above when taken together sufficiently establish the dimensions listed (A) to (K) at the beginning of this chapter. Building off this critical literature I now turn to Mill's primary texts in the second chapter to outline more completely Mill's imperial democratization and good governance theorem.

Chapter 2

Mill's Imperial Democratization Theorem

In this chapter I focus on Mill's primary texts to show that Mill brings together ideas of imperialism, democracy, and principles of good governance to articulate a comprehensive imperial democratization and good governance theorem. It is remarkable to me how this piece of Mill's liberal imperialism has not been emphasized in scholarship on Mill given that in *Considerations* he builds a democratization framework in a political and social scientific manner which is not only completely original among those thinkers privileged in the Western canon, but also remained unrivalled as a work of this type until the late 20th century construction of 'democratization' as a specialized discipline of political science.[123] This field includes further specializations such as transitology, the study of a polity transitioning from one system of government to another. Transition from one form of governance to another is a theme Mill gave special attention to in his theorem.

This absence of attention is also noteworthy given the attention one of Mill's influences and contemporaries, Alexis de Tocqueville who wrote the classic *Democracy in America*, has received in the contemporary democratization field. Tocqueville has received such attention even though he had nothing close to the type of democratization theorem one finds in Mill. Although democratization literature turns to Tocqueville for ideas on civic culture and civic virtue, Mill's thought is also rich in similar notions. The place of Tocqueville and Mill in contemporary democratization literature is beyond the scope of this thesis so I limit myself below to explicating Mill's theorem.

I proceed in outlining Mill's theorem by analyzing and interpreting Mill's three most relevant texts. The most pertinent primary works are *Considerations on Representative Government* (1861),[124] "A Few Words on Non-Intervention" (1859)[125], and the essay "Civilization" (1836).[126] These are listed in the order by which each is discussed in this chapter with *Considerations* being first and most extensively discussed because it is the latest of these works, the longest of these works, and it constitutes the most explicit and extensive treatise by Mill on his extensive and tightly packaged imperial democratization and good governance theorem.

Considerations on Representative Government: Treatise of a Theorem

My approach to *Considerations* is not to list all the imperial dimensions that are employed within the theorem, as the bulk of these are identified in my first chapter, but to theorize how such various imperial dimensions identified by the critical literature are brought together by Mill in *Considerations* to formulate his imperial democratization and good governance theorem. Note that Mill thinks that his theorem should guide the British Empire in its rule of dependencies around the globe.[127] This, combined with the fact that Mill sees his doctrine as acceptable and necessary to the two dominant British political camps of his day, forms the basis on which I frame Mill's theorem as a transcendental doctrine. Mill himself wrote in the preface of *Considerations* that the principles employed in *Considerations* are those for which he had been "working up during the greater part" of his life; and Mill adds that these principles articulate a doctrine which could and should be "adopted by either Liberal or Conservative without renouncing anything which he really feels to be valuable in his own creed."[128] A theory and practice of imperialism for the ends of Mill's vision of civilizational progress are at the core of this doctrine.

There are three aspects to this transcendental quality of Mill's theorem for guiding humanity to Mill's particular ideal of civilizational progress which correspond to the three elements Mill brings together in forming the theorem: imperialism, democracy, and good governance. Regarding the first (imperialism), partisan Conservatives and partisan Liberals could both support an imperial practice of ruling non-civilized others as a means of improving humanity. Regarding the second (democracy), Conservatives and Liberals could both support moving others, albeit gradually through stages and transitions by satisfying the proper conditions, to a British model of representative government.[129] What Mill means by representative government is what we call today a liberal-democratic system including a constitutional and institutional package that includes an electoral process, the rule of law, a separation of powers between the executive, legislative, and judicial branches of government, as well as a mass press orchestrated by intellectuals which together constitute a particular system of government.[130] The third is good governance; Liberals and Conservatives could both support principles of good governance meaning that a nation should have the appropriate and effective form of governance in correspondence to its civilizational character.[131] To elaborate, this would be the form of government that best improves the overall civilizational quality of the people over which government operates.[132]

Each of the three elements and transcendental aspects will be illustrated as I work through *Considerations*. I do so to show how Mill brings these three elements and aspects together as an imperial democratization and good governance theorem which Mill sees as a practical guidebook on how to use European, especially British, power and influence to move humanity to civilizational progress.[133] The three elements of Mill's imperial democratization and good governance theorem may seem an awkward mix today because languages and practices of democracy and good governance are often erroneously presumed to be mutually exclusive from theories and practices of imperialism, but they are often intricately related.[134] Regardless of the contentiousness of this point generally I aim merely to illuminate that these three elements fit together in Mill's theorem.

There are three sections to my presentation of *Considerations* as Mill's treatise on his theorem. First I provide a sketch of seven basic forms of government with which Mill is concerned. These are worth keeping in view in endeavoring to understand Mill's theorem. Second, I outline the first four chapters of *Considerations* in turn which, when taken together, form the architecture of Mill's theorem. Third I discuss the last three chapters of *Considerations* which further highlight issues in relation to Mill's theorem and *Considerations* as a treatise of this theorem.

Forms of Government: Seven Basic Types

For Mill, there are seven basic forms of government that he sees as operating in modern circumstances. These forms work as weapons against or as a set of tools for the civilizational progress of humanity. These forms from Mill's perspective are the following types from worst to best with their functional quality as a civilizing tool noted with each:[135]

(1) Native anarchy is, for Mill, a form of government that is never appropriate and is the most evil and horrible state of "rude" and "savage" existence that any person or collective of peoples could live.

(2) Native malevolent despotism, according to Mill, is also never appropriate according to Mill because it is barely better than the first.

(3) Native benevolent self-despotism, according to Mill, requires an indigenous leader of extraordinary genius and Mill asserts that this is too rare a circumstance to ever be considered an option as an appropriate form of government.

(4) Malevolent despotism by foreign superior peoples is a form of government that, for Mill, is problematic. It is a useful form of government for teaching non-civilized nations obedience through enslavement, especially "savages" who according to Mill sometimes have no other means of improvement. The problem for Mill is that this form of government is not conducive to the character and progress of the superior peoples doing the governing and therefore is not a good form of government for the imperial civilizing project.

(5) Benevolent despotism by a foreign civilized and superior people is a form that Mill sees as a practical option and required in many contingent cases in his era, such as in "Hindustan," because it improves both the "civilized" and the "non-civilized". It teaches the latter obedience with only as much force as necessary and the former carry out progress consciously and nobly by imperially governing with the explicit purpose of

"gradually" teaching inferiors through "guidance" how to "walk alone" as liberal moderns with a system of representative government.

(6) Local administrative self-government under an imperial sovereign authority is a step up from benevolent despotism. Under local administrative self-government, the local population is, or has become "civilized" and therefore is ready, willing, and able to conduct itself responsibly enough to hold many local jurisdictional powers. For Mill this provides good training in governing oneself because it enables daily practices which form the character necessary to further acquire and maintain representative government while still being under the guidance of a "superior" people capable of intricately interfering and intervening with their protectorate indigenous populations when required.

(7) Representative government. Ideally, this is the best from of government for humanity in modernity but it is only and necessarily appropriate for civilized nations.

The sketch above encapsulates the forms of government Mill has in view in *Considerations* when he builds his imperial democratization and good governance theorem. *Considerations* is a work divided into 18 chapters. The chapters I discuss here include the first four (chapters 1-4) and then the last three (chapters 16-18). These chapters are selected not only because they are the ones that fit with my concern regarding Mill's theorem but also because these are the chapters that frame *Considerations* itself, as the middle chapters largely discuss questions of institutional design taking the principles and validity claims brought together in the other seven chapters for granted. Recall that the first four chapters constitute the architecture of Mill's theorem. It is worthwhile to note the titles of each chapter as I discuss them in chronological order because they inform what is being laid down in each procedural piece of architectural logic from which Mill systematically builds his theorem.

The Architecture of the Theorem

The first chapter, "To What Extent Forms of Government are a Matter of Choice," is key to understanding the imperial democratization and good governance theorem since it sets out three conditions that penetrate the rest of the theorem. I refer to these conditions as Mill's will and ability clause because embedded within the core of these conditions, both individually and as set of related conditions is a pseudo factual norm. This is Mill's validity claim that peoples must be at least willing but usually ready, able, and willing to conduct themselves in the particular ways that are required and conducive to acquiring and maintaining a single, particular, and appropriate form of government. I will show in more depth below that for Mill the appropriate form of government is that which fits a particular people's civilizational state ("savage", "barbarian", or "civilized") meaning it best protects and promotes civilizational progress for themselves and for humankind.[136] In fact this is Mill's meaning of good governance.[137]

The significance of these conditions is recognized by Mill himself when he explicitly asserts that the "failure of any of these conditions renders a form of government, whatever favourable promise it may otherwise hold out, unsuitable to the particular case."[138] Mill provides these conditions most succinctly when he writes:

> ...representative, like any other government, must be unsuitable in any case in which it cannot permanently subsist—*i.e.* in which it does not fulfil the three fundamental conditions enumerated in the first chapter. These were—1. That the people should be willing to receive it. 2. That they should be willing and able to do what is necessary for its preservation. 3. That they should be willing and be able to fulfill the duties and discharge the functions which it imposes on them.[139]

Beyond what has been explicated above thus far, there are three things that need to be illustrated regarding the will and ability clause. First, is that Mill's civilizational language is at the core of these conditions. Second, is that these conditions and the civilizational language intrinsic to them form the basis by which Mill concludes that forms of government are a matter of choice for the civilized but are not a matter of choice for the non-civilized.[140] Third is that the will and ability clause in excluding the non-civilized from choosing forms of government, opens up the non-civilized to the justification of foreign force to imperially provide the right forms of government. To illustrate these three points and how they relate to each other it is valuable to see each condition laid out in Mill's own words as a first move in chapter one of *Considerations*.

Mill's original explication of condition (1), that the people must be willing to receive the form of government in question is thus:

> The first obstacle, the repugnance of the people to the particular form of government, needs little illustration, because it never can in theory have been overlooked. The case is of perpetual occurrence. Nothing but foreign force would induce a tribe of North American Indians to submit to the restraints of a regular and civilized government....There are nations who will not voluntarily submit to any government but that of certain families, which have from time immemorial had the privilege of supplying them with chiefs. Some nations could not, except by foreign conquest, be made to endure a monarchy; others are equally averse to a republic. The hindrance often amounts, for the time being, to impracticability.[141]

For Mill, the various indigenous polities of North America in his day[142] were a pertinent example of "savages" in which forms of government are not a matter of choice because they are, for now, too "repugnant" of a civilization to improve through imperial governance.[143] For Mill, these polities had not yet learned the first lesson of civilization, obedience.[144] Furthermore, these polities did not even want the proper forms of governance from the "civilized" that could "improve" them.[145]

Upon laying out the first condition Mill moves on to the next condition of the will and ability clause and theorizes cases in which condition one is satisfied, meaning the "non-civilized" in question must at least want, or in Mill's words "will", the proper form of government. Mill writes that even with condition one being satisfied people "must be ready, willing, and able to preserve" the form of government in question. Mill's original explication of this second condition is thus:

> But there are also cases in which, though not averse to a form of government—possibly even desiring it—a people may be unwilling or unable to fulfil its conditions. They may be incapable of fulfilling such of them as are necessary to keep the government even in nominal existence. Thus a people may prefer a free government, but if, from indolence, or carelessness, or cowardice, or want of public spirit, they are unequal to the exertions necessary for preserving it; if they will not fight for it when it is directly attacked; if they can be deluded by the artifices used to cheat them out of it; if by momentary discouragement, or temporary panic, or a fit of enthusiasm for an individual, they can be induced to lay their liberties at the feet even of a great man, or trust him with powers which enable him to subvert their institutions; in all these cases they are more or less unfit for liberty: and though it may be for their good to have had it even for a short time, they are unlikely long to enjoy it.[146]

Mill then moves on to the third condition of the will and ability clause, asserting that even in cases when conditions one and two are not met (the nation must will and desire the form of government and must preserve the form of government) the people must also satisfy the third condition. The third condition is that they must be ready, willing, and able to discharge the duties required of the form of government in question[147]. Regarding this third condition, Mill says the non-civilized are unfit because "they may be unwilling or unable to fulfil the duties which a particular form of government requires of them."[148]

Following the placement of these conditions Mill then notes what he believes to follow from these conditions, particularly the third. Mill writes that for "a rude people" to be ruled by a foreign civilized nation in a way that is "really advantageous" to them it will be required that the "civilized" ruler will be "in a considerable degree despotic." Mill elaborates that this advantageous despotism will impose "a great amount of forcible restraint upon their actions." The relationship between the prescription of imperial despotism and the will and ability clause is emphasized by Mill when he writes that "a people must be considered unfit for more than a limited and qualified freedom, who will not co-operate actively with the law and the public authorities, in the repression of evil-doers." In addition to the prescription of despotic rule of the non-civilized by the civilized, Mill's civilizational language is further invoked when Mill elaborates that those "who are more disposed to shelter a criminal than to apprehend him; who, like the Hindoos will perjure themselves to screen the man who has robbed them" require that the ruling "authorities should be armed with much sterner powers of repression than elsewhere."[149] This is because the "first indispensable requisites of civilized life have nothing else to rest on."[150]

The first chapter firmly establishes the will and ability clause which is the first architectural piece of Mill's imperial democratization and good governance theorem. These conditions draw boundaries which divide the "civilized" from the "non-civilized." There are those inside these boundaries, "civilized" peoples, who satisfy all conditions and can choose their forms of government. And there are those outside these boundaries, the "non-civilized", who do not satisfy the conditions of the will and ability clause and therefore cannot choose their own forms of government. For Mill the civilized are most exemplified in modern times by the British nation[151] and the non-civilized are most exemplified by the "Hindoos" of "Hindustan" and the "North American Indians."[152]

The second chapter titled "The Criterion of a Good Form of Government" is the second piece of architecture which, building off of the will and ability clause explicated above, is necessary for understanding what Mill means by "appropriate form of government" and what Mill means by "principles of good governance," which along with imperialism and democracy form one crucial element of the theorem. In this chapter Mill has two main components to his conception of the criterion of a good form of government. The first is institutional and the second is socio-cultural. Before laying out each component Mill outlines the basic metaphysical axis upon which his two pronged criterion of good government is built.[153]

Mill begins by arguing that it is most "philosophically correct" if one is to provide a "first commencement of scientific precision to the notion of good government" to say that the best form of government is that which is "most conducive to progress."[154] By progress Mill means civilizational improvement, both material and moral.[155] In outlining progress as the metaphysical axis upon which the goodness of a form of government rests, Mill deconstructs the notion of the good polity into two social exigencies: progress and order.

The first component (the institutional) is born out of Mill's understanding of the relationship between progress and order. In his discussion of the two exigencies Mill takes order to mean obedience and argues that progress necessarily includes order but order does not necessarily include progress and emphasizes the importance of the relationship between the two.[156] The importance of this relationship for Mill is twofold.

First, as implied above, is that you cannot have progress without the appropriate forms of order.[157] Second, and related to the first, is that both too much order and too little order can be an obstacle to progress[158] in three ways: by preventing progress and maintaining a stationary existence, by instigating regress, or by not instigating as much progress as could be the case with an alternative quantity or quality of order.[159] Recall that Mill assumes a spatial-temporal model in which historical movement has only three possibilities along a linear axis: to regress, to stay stationary, or to progress.[160] Hence the importance for Mill in having the right institutionalized system of order (security of property, juridical institutions, etc.) to promote progress.[161] In essence, forms of government are systems of order and therefore work for or against improving civilizational progress.

Mill qualifies his account of the criterion of a good form of government arguing that though "metaphysically defensible" progress in itself is too inapt a notion upon which such a criterion could rest.[162] Mill then argues that it is the types of human character rather than merely the types of external institutionalized order that constitute the requisites of good government. This is thus the second component, the socio-cultural component, to Mill's criterion of a good government.[163] This socio-cultural component of Mill's criterion of a good form of government is simply stated by Mill when he writes:

> If we ask ourselves on what causes and conditions good government in all its senses, from the humblest to the most exalted, depends, we find that the principal of them, the one which transcends all others, is the qualities of the human beings composing the society over which government is exercised.[164]

These two different components (institutional and socio-cultural) of Mill's criterion of a good form of government that is built on his metaphysical axis of progress are brought together by Mill when he writes:

> We may consider, then, as one criterion of the goodness of a government, the degree in which it tends to increase the sum of good qualities in the governed, collectively and individually; since besides that their well-being is the sole object of government, their good qualities supply the moving force [that] works the machinery. This leaves, as the other constituent element of the merit of a government, the quality of the machinery itself; that is, the degree in which it is adapted to take advantage of the amount of good qualities which may at any time exist, and make them instrumental to the right purposes.[165]

Once Mill has outlined what he means by good governance and appropriate forms of government, or appropriate systems of order, he provides the major nexus point of contact between the first chapter (the assertion of the will and ability clause), this second chapter (asserting the meaning of good governance and appropriate forms of government), and the next two chapters that I discuss below (chapter three which asserts that representative government is the ideal form of government and chapter four which reemphasizes how the previous chapters fit together). This nexus point of contact is Mill's imperial democratization approach succinctly explicated in the second chapter when Mill writes in a crucial passage:

> A despotism, which may tame the savage, will, in so far as it is a despotism, only confirm the slaves in their incapacities. Yet a government under their own control would be entirely unmanageable by them. Their improvement cannot come from themselves, but must be superinduced from without. The step which they have to take, and their only path to improvement, is to be raised from a government of will to one of law. They have to be taught self-government, and this, in its initial stage, means the capacity to act on general instructions. What they require is not a government of force, but one of guidance. Being, however, in too low a state to yield to the guidance of any but those to whom they look up as the possessors of force, the sort of government fittest for them is one which possesses force, but seldom uses it: a parental despotism or aristocracy, resembling the St. Simonian form of socialism; maintaining a general superintendence over all operations of

society, so as to keep before each the sense of a present force sufficient to compel his obedience to the rule laid down, but which, owing to the impossibility of descending to regulate all the minutiae of industry and life, necessarily leaves and induces individuals to do much of themselves. This, which may be termed *the government of leading strings*, seems to be the one required to carry such a people the most rapidly through the next necessary step in social progress...*leading-strings are only admissible as a means of gradually training the people to walk alone.*[166]

It is worth noting that Mill here refers to benevolent despotism (guiding the savage towards progress) as a particular form of government in contrast to malevolent despotism (forming a slave capacity for the purpose of perpetual exploitation). The distinction between the two forms of despotism has two lines of differentiation. The first line is a matter of when force is used (in the case of benevolent despotism only when necessary) and the second is a matter of why force is used (in the case of benevolent despotism only to guide the non-civilized and therefore humanity to progress).

Of course both lines of differentiation are dependent on the superior peoples' ability to judge well and, more fundamentally, they depend on the modular conceptions of civilization and progress that Mill employs or in other words, the modular conceptions of civilization and progress employed by the superior peoples. Because Mill's imperial democratization approach relies so much on superior peoples' judgment, *Considerations* is Mill's attempt to provide a theorem to guide this judgment and carry out practical action. The purpose of his theorem is perhaps best encapsulated at the end of the second chapter when Mill writes in another crucial passage thus:

It is, then impossible to understand the question of the adaptation of forms of government to states of society, without taking into account not only the next step, but all the steps which society has yet to make; both those which can be foreseen, and the far wider indefinite range which is at present out of sight. It follows, that to judge of the merits of forms of government, an ideal must be constructed of the form of government most eligible in itself, that is, which, if the necessary conditions existed for giving effect to its beneficial tendencies, would, more than all others, favour and promote not some one improvement, but all forms and degrees of it. This having been done, we must consider what are the mental conditions of all sorts, necessary to enable this government to realize its tendencies, and what therefore, are the various defects by which a people is made incapable of reaping its benefits. *It would then be possible to construct a theorem of circumstances in which that form of government may wisely be introduced, and also to judge in cases in which it had better not be introduced, what inferior forms of polity will best carry those communities through the intermediate stages which they must traverse before they can become fit for the best form of government.*[167]

As shown by the passages above this important second chapter in itself, informed by the will and ability clause and the civilizational language that is intrinsic to it, outlines that Mill is systematically putting together a practical framework for imperially democratizing the non-civilized through the power of the civilized and their knowledge of principles of good governance. This framework is meant to aid the civilized in such a project.[168] And it is intended to be a social scientific framework that plugs into its calculations a consideration of vast and complex circumstantial inputs including preconditions, conditions, steps, intermediate stages, transitions, local circumstances, and appropriate forms of government for local circumstances including assessment of civilizational culture and material development. These are the types of considerations that go into contemporary democratization frameworks produced in the late 20th century. Mill's conclusion of this chapter posits that this "ideally best form of government" alluded to at the end of the passage above will be "found in some one or other variety of the Representative System."[169]

The third chapter titled that the "Ideally Best Form of Government is Representative Government" further discusses the concept of good despotism in relation to varieties of human character and civilizational conditions. There are four points in this third piece of Mill's architecture to be noted before moving on to the fourth chapter.

First, Mill emphasizes the difference between good despotism as a step and good despotism as an ideal. Mill sees the former as a temporary measure and step consistent with the criterion of good governance in contrast to the claim that if a good despot could be ensured then despotic monarchy would be the best form of government. Mill endorses the good despotism as a realistic step and rejects the idealization of good despotism mainly because Mill thinks representative government and not good despotism is the only form of government compatible with civilizational character; representative government was also what England had at the time.

Second, and related to the first, is that for Mill an application of good despotism would send an advanced nation like England into regressive decline.[170] This concern with historical regress is present when Mill argues that to say that good despotism is the best form of government for the civilized is to say "if the whole testimony of human history is worth anything" that "the era of national decline has arrived."[171] Mill continues:

> [Arrived]…that is, if the nation had ever attained anything to decline from. If it has never risen above the condition of an Oriental people…it continues to stagnate. But if like Greece or Rome, it had realized anything higher, through the energy, patriotism, and enlargement of mind, which as national qualities are the fruits soley of freedom, it relapses in a few generations into the Oriental state. And that state does not mean stupid tranquility, with security against change for the worse; it often means being overrun, conquered, and reduced to domestic slavery, either by a stronger despot, or by the nearest barbarous people who retain along with their savage rudeness the energies of freedom.[172]

Third, Mill provides one major criterion of the ideal best form government and two principles upon which the superiority of popular government rests; Mill narrows popular government down to representative government in this chapter. Mill states that the ideally best form of government "is not one which is practicable or eligible in all states of civilization," but rather the one which is practical and eligible in the best state of civilization that exists in the circumstances of the present. Mill viewed the English as the best civilization of his day and representative government as the best form of government for the civilized.[173] The two principles upon which the superiority of popular government rests are, firstly, that "the rights and interests of every or any person are only secure from being disregarded, when the person interested is himself able, and habitually disposed, to stand-up for them",—this is an expression of the will and ability clause presuming a civilized context. The second principle is that under popular government, prosperity more efficiently attains a greater height and is more widely diffused (recall that material development is important to civilizational progress).[174]

It is worth noting two values Mill sees in the present application of these two principles. People can only walk alone and be secure from the evil of others if they are "self-protecting" (a moral, material, and military value) and "self-dependent" (a moral, material, and economic value).[175] For Mill, this all culminates into the meaning of walking alone which is that people walk alone when they are "relying in what they themselves can do, either separately or in concert, rather than what others do for them."[176]

It is important to emphasize that walking alone must be an action that is within the boundaries drawn by the will and ability clause. For Mill, it is not possible nor acceptable to walk alone in a way that deviates outside of the three conditions of the will and ability clause nor away from Mill's modular notions of civilization and progress.[177] For example the civilized cannot walk alone by choosing a government that is not representative government; this would be a regressive act antithetical to the rational and able conduct that is necessarily intrinsic to civilizational character.[178] And the "non-civilized" cannot learn to walk alone by governing themselves or by being governed in a way that is different than that one particular form of government that the inferior peoples need according to Mill's theorem. A worthwhile problem of Mill's thought for further consideration is how it is that the civilized can supposedly choose forms of government yet must choose representative government by virtue of being civilized? It seems that in relation to many of the meanings of the term "choice" that forms of government are a not actually a matter of choice for the civilized in the context of Mill's logic.

On the fourth point, Mill divides the comparison of good despotism versus representative government to "a still more fundamental one" which is thus:

> which of the two common types of character, for the general good of humanity, it is most desirable to predominate—the active, or the passive type; that which struggles against evils, or that which endures them; that which bends to circumstances, or that which endeavors to make circumstances bend to itself.[179]

This division of humanity into two character types maps on to Mill's binary form of civilizational language in that the civilized have an active character and the non-civilized have a passive character.[180] Furthermore each character type, and their corresponding civilization, promote or work against three varieties of mental excellence: intellectual, practical, and moral.[181] This mix of relationships between character types, civilizational states, and varieties of mental excellence being put together by Mill in this third chapter is perhaps best exemplified in the passage below:

> In proportion as success in life is seen or believed to be the fruit of fatality or accident and not of exertion, in that same ratio does envy develope itself as a point of national character. The most envious of all mankind are the Orientals. In Oriental moralists, in Oriental tales, the envious man is markedly prominent. In real life, he is the terror of all who possess anything desirable, be it a palace, a handsome child, or even good health and spirits: the supposed effect of his mere look constitutes the all-pervading superstition of the evil eye. Next to Orientals in envy, as in activity are some of the Southern Europeans. The Spaniards pursued all their great men with it, embittered their lives, and generally succeeded in

putting an early stop to their successes. With the French, who are essentially a southern people, the double education of despotism and Catholicism has, in spite of their impulsive temperament, made submission and endurance the common character of the people, and their most received notion of wisdom and excellence: and if envy of one another, and of all superiority, is not more rife among them than it is, the circumstance must be ascribed to the many valuable counteracting elements in the French character, and most of all to the great individual energy which, though less persistent and more intermittent than in the self-helping and struggling Anglo-Saxons, has nevertheless manifested itself among the French in nearly every direction in which the operation of their institutions has been favourable to it.[182]

Mill's typology of humanity is outlined here along a continuum from passive to active which largely parallels his continuum of civilized and non-civilized. The one exception is that Mill sometimes frames "savages" as being below the passive non-civilized nations due to too much rude activeness; as not having the mature discipline needed for the material development that is necessary to moral development and civilizational progress. The first lesson of civilization is, after all, obedience which is a lesson of discipline and a lesson that Mill asserts has not been learned by "North American Indians." Mill's view of Anglo character being the most civilized of modern times is also clearly asserted above, but is also further outlined when he writes that the striving "go-ahead character of England and the United States" in itself is the "foundation of the best hopes for the general improvement of mankind."[183] Mill emphasizes this special historical character of these two countries when he compares it to the character of France, a country and nation that Mill considers among the best three civilizations in the modern world. In this comparison Mill writes:

It has been acutely remarked, that whenever anything goes amiss, the habitual impulse of French people is to say, "Il faut de la patience;" and of English people, "What a shame." The people who think it a shame when anything goes wrong— who rush to the conclusion that the evil could and ought to have been prevented, are those who, in the long run, do most to make the world better.[184]

For Mill the majority of humanity carries an inactive form of character; this is a point explicitly made in this third chapter[185] and this illuminates why his imperial democratization and good governance theorem is seen as an aid to civilizational progress. Mill concludes this third chapter by stating that "there can be no doubt that the passive character is favoured by the government of one or a few, and the active self-helping type by that of the Many."[186] Popular and democratic representative government becomes the ideally best form of government rather than the ancient Athenian model of government mainly because this is the best that the circumstances of industrial modernity allow and it is the form of government practiced by the world's most advanced nation, England. Hence, this third piece of architecture of Mill's theorem is the one that most strongly infuses and ties the element of democracy with imperialism and good governance.[187]

The last of the first four chapters titled "Under What Social Conditions Representative Government is Inapplicable" which in combination with the previous three chapters constitute what I consider to be the architecture of Mill's theorem, does not, in itself, add any new central component to this architecture.[188] Rather this chapter summarizes what Mill believes he has established in the first three chapters. Not surprisingly then the first two points Mill reiterates in this chapter are, first, that representative government is the "ideal type of the most perfect polity" and second that representative government, "like any form of government", is only suitable for those who satisfy the will and ability clause which in the case of representative government are only and necessarily the civilized. Mill restates the three conditions of the will and ability clause here.[189]

Mill does outline conditions when representative government cannot permanently exist. With this outline, however, when Mill goes through cases where representative government might possibly exist but in which some other form of government would be preferable (such as good despotism) Mill does not add detail. Rather Mill refers to the cases that have already been discussed in the previous chapters referring therefore to cases such as "North American Indians" who Mill frames as "savages" and "Hindoos" who Mill frames as "barbarians."

Another point that Mill reiterates in this fourth chapter is that those with a passive character (the non-civilized) are unfit for representative government.[190] And Mill argues that even if the best individuals of a passive society could rule despotically they would likely reflect the "defects of national character", the "mere ignorance", and "the deficiency of mental cultivation" found in the people themselves. In ending the fourth chapter Mill also restates how imperialism, democracy, and good governance fit together into an imperial democratization approach, or in Mill's words his "government of leading strings", that tie together the four chapters as the architecture of his theorem. He writes here:

> From the general weakness of the people or of the state of civilization, the One and his counsellors, or the Few, are not likely to be habitually exempt; except in the case of their being foreigners, belonging to a superior people or more advanced state of society. Then, indeed, the rulers may be, to almost any extent, superior in civilization to those over whom they rule; and subjection to a foreign government of this description, notwithstanding its inevitable evils, is often of the greatest advantage to a people, carrying them rapidly through several stages of progress, and clearing away obstacles to improvement which might have lasted indefinitely if the subject population had been left unassisted to its native tendencies and chances. In a country not under the dominion of foreigners, the only cause adequate to producing similar benefits is the rare accident of a monarch genius.[191]

Mill's theorem, encapsulated well by the passage above is systematically built in the first four chapters of *Considerations*. Before departing from *Considerations* I discuss the last three chapters of *Consideration*s because together they further illuminate the points above and enrich our understanding of Mill's theorem.

Nationality, Federalism, and British Imperial Order

In chapter 16 titled "Of Nationality" Mill provides an account of what he means by "nation" and the "sentiment of nationality."[192] For Mill, "a portion of mankind may be said to constitute" a nationality "if they are united among themselves by common sympathies" which make them "co-operate with each other more willingly than with other people" and that they desire a government "by themselves or a portion of themselves", exclusively.[193] This is worth noting since Mill often refers to civilizations, societies, peoples, barbarians, and savages as nations but also thinks of nationality as a quality some peoples have (the civilized) and some peoples do not have (the "non-civilized"), or as a continuum of gradations running in linear progression from the lower rung of non-civilized to the higher rung of civilized. Moreover, Mill makes a number of substantive claims that operate within his theorem. One is that free institutions are impossible in a country made up of different nationalities.[194] Another is that experience proves that it is possible for one nationality to be absorbed into another.[195]

Since it is impossible for a country to have multiple nations Mill thinks it is often the case that the stronger of the nations, the better civilization with the more active character, should absorb weaker nations so that the latter can acquire the beneficial qualities of the former,[196] or as Mill puts it, the "excellences of all its progenitors."[197] Mill also provides an instructional scheme in this chapter describing when nationality absorption should take place and he goes through cases where "the greatest obstacles exist to blending nationalities."[198] Mill's diagnosis of such obstacles to "nationality blending" leads him to discuss federalism as a solution. Mill thinks federations "might usefully tie multiple nations together" but he sees it as problematic and ends this chapter on nationality on this broad point. Federalism, then, is the subject of Mill's next chapter.[199]

I need not go into extensive depth regarding Mill's work on federalism in chapter 17 titled "Of Federal Representative Government."[200] I merely want to note the way that Mill's discussion of federalism takes place in the context of his imperial democratization and good governance theorem. First it is only the non-civilized nations that need federations because, after all, the civilized can walk alone. For Mill federations are formed to enable nations who cannot be blended but who have enough common sympathies to co-operate in self-defense. The larger benefit of federalism for Mill is that it results in a "diminishing of petty states" and therefore the multiplication of successful federations is "always beneficial to the world."[201] This latter point, interestingly, gestures towards a historical dialectic leading towards a more integrated and orderly world system. Mill, taking the U.S. mode of federation as the best of two models, marvels at the U.S. achievement of a Supreme Court which he sees as the basis for a model of an "International Tribunal" which Mill describes as one of the most important "prominent wants of civilized society."[202] The last chapter illuminates more clearly the way in which Mill conceptualizes an international tribunal as an institution of European, especially British, imperial governance.

In the final chapter of *Considerations*, chapter 18 titled "Of the Government of Dependencies by a Free State," Mill writes that free states "may possess dependencies" and so "it is an important question how such dependencies ought to be governed."[203] Mill divides dependencies into two classes. The first are "civilized" and are ripe for representative government, Mill provides examples of settler colonies such as Austrailia and the British North American colonies which he sees as similar in "race" to the English; by "race" I take Mill to be employing a cultural concept in an extensively ethnocentric way.[204] And the second are "non-civilized" and are not ripe for representative government; Mill sees these as being composed of people more dissimilar in "race" than the English and points to "Hindustan" as his example. Discussing the former first, Mill describes English practice as realizing the "true principle in government" and distinguishes between the vicious colonialism of the past, "once common to all Europe... but not yet completely relinquished by any other people,"[205] from the "good" imperialism of England of his day where interference into internal affairs is kept minimal and carried out only when necessary.

I will not recount Mill's case for this practice of true government and good imperial policy, but I will emphasize that this policy of "good" imperialism applied to Great Britain's colonies of "European Race" meant that the settler communities of these colonies were allowed the "fullest measure of self-government" with representative institutions.[206] For Mill the internal is important as he sees it as an imperative of good imperial policy that the Crown and the British Parliament have a veto to exercise on rare occasions when an internal issue concerns the empire, and not solely the particular colony.[207] Mill sees the "liberal construction" of this distinction between imperial versus colonial questions as established in English practice while simultaneously revealing that even the civilized colonies are not to be beyond the yoke of imperial governance from England. Mill writes in support of his claims and of this distinction:

the whole of the unappropriated lands in the regions behind our American and Australian colonies, have been given up to the uncontrolled disposal of the colonial communities; though they might, without injustice, have been kept in the hands of the Imperial Government, to be administered for the greatest advantage of future emigrants from all parts of the empire. Every colony has thus as full power over its own affairs, as it could have if it were a member of even the loosest federation; and much fuller than would belong to it under the Constitution of the United States, being free even to tax at its pleasure the commodities imported from the mother country. Their union with Great Britain is the slightest kind of federal union; but not a strictly equal federation, the mother country retaining itself the powers of a Federal Government, though reduced in practice to their very narrowest limits. This inequality is, of course, as far as   it goes, a disadvantage to the dependencies, which have no voice in foreign policy, but are bound by the decisions of the superior country. They are compelled to join England in war, without being any way consulted previous to engaging in it.[208]

Following this, Mill rejects the vision of a world federation where there are no longer dependencies stating that such a vision is inconsistent with rational principles of government. Mill argues that it is British imperial governance which is consistent with rational principles of governance, as described in relation to the civilized dependencies by Mill above, because it best maintains the present bond among civilized peoples and best provides a "step towards universal peace and friendly cooperation among nations."[209] Mother countries exclusively decide questions of war and peace. Of course, since many matters can be subsumed as a question of war and peace this limitation on the internal affairs of a settler colony may not be, despite Mill's explicit claims to the contrary, very limiting.

Mill ends this chapter, and *Considerations*, by considering the governance of "non-civilized" dependencies which are not fit for representative government.[210] Using India as the primary example, Mill thinks colonialism is for much of humanity a universal condition and that it is the duty of the civilized with such dependencies to not govern these dependencies directly *via* their own government who may be merely engaged in malevolent despotism but to provide these countries with good rulers. It is worth noting that Mill famously advocated as a public intellectual and as an MP that his employer, the East India Company, was a good ruler of India and that the English Parliament would make a poor ruler of India. This is an experience and an issue that likely informs this particular distinction between rule by foreign peoples and rule by foreign governors.[211] Regardless, Mill's theorem is meant to provide a framework for superior peoples, such as the English, to use in providing a proper ruler for inferior peoples for the ends of civilizational progress.[212]

I now turn to two earlier texts relevant to this doctrine to, among other things, further illustrate the role of English exceptionalism and civilizational progress in Mill's theorem. These shorter and earlier Mill texts are "A Few Words on Non-Intervention" published in 1859 and "Civilization" published in 1836.

"A Few Words on Non-Intervention": The Theorem in Context

Mill, within two years prior to the publication of *Considerations*, stated in his 1859 article "A Few Words on Non-intervention" that:

> There are few questions which more require to be taken in hand by ethical and political philosophers, with a view to establish some rule or criterion whereby the justifiableness of intervening in the affairs of other countries, and (what is sometimes as questionable) the justifiableness of refraining from intervention, may be brought to a definite and rational test."[213]

Mill's theorem at the core of *Considerations* lays out such rational tests in regards to intervention by superior civilized nations into the affairs of inferior non-civilized nations by combining Mill's will and ability clause with his criterion of good governance and his imperial democratization program. The meta-normative end of both *Considerations* and

"A Few Words on Non-Intervention" is "civilizational progress" and both texts advocate intervention as a means of supporting this end.

Mill's article, "A Few Words on Non-Intervention" (1859), was written in response to a diplomatic row between Britain and France over a plan to construct the Suez Canal. This incident broke-out because France, during a conference at Constantinople in 1859 was seeking to acquire rights to move forward on ambitious plans to have a French firm build the Suez Canal in Egypt. The British Prime Minister at the time diplomatically opposed the notion of a French firm obtaining the rights of such a project which, if successful, had large implications and significant value for rival European empires in terms of economic trade and military strategy; hence concerns and diplomatic politics over the project.[214]

I will not go into the details of this event but I want to note the obvious fact that the context of this issue possessed global, imperial, and colonial dimensions that involve, in Mill's phraseology, superior civilized nations (England and France) as well as inferior dependencies (Egypt). At this time Egypt was a protectorate of the Ottoman empire soon to be briefly occupied by France before becoming a British protectorate. Against this backdrop, or in other words in the practical context of this diplomatic row, I argue that we get a partial glimpse of Mill's theorem in action.

To further contextualize the article it is worth outlining three purposes Mill had in writing it. One purpose of the article was to espouse his own viewpoint of what the English government's position and diplomatic language should be regarding the likely commencement of the French project in Egypt.[215] Mill opposed the English Prime Minister's handling of the issue[216] but also defended the true greatness of the English character against Continental criticism,[217] and at the same time defended the validity of French concerns over English character given the misleading language and action of the English Prime Minister.[218] Mill viewed a successful Suez Canal project as an act which would promote and protect civilizational progress and English opposition to such a project as an act which posed an unnecessary obstacle to civilizational progress.[219]

Another purpose for Mill was to make two distinctions. One distinction was between the character of English people versus the character of the English politicians whom Mill disagreed with in this article.[220] And second is the distinction between the established practices of England versus the poor judgment of one English individual who happened to be the Prime Minister in one moment in history acting on one issue of foreign policy.[221]

Mill's third purpose with the article was to take the opportunity against the backdrop of this event, to publicize his position on two large ethical topics of foreign policy. One was to reconsider the doctrine and practice of non-intervention; specifically on the proper duties, limits, and liberties in terms of the politics on the use of force against other nations.[222] Mill's concern over this question was for England specifically, civilized nations generally, and to categorically assert that non-civilized nations are not protected by the norms of such a doctrine. The second ethical topic was on whether superior civilized nations could and should rule inferior non-civilized nations.[223] The latter took the form of a defense of British rule of India and French rule of Algeria and also played a prominent role in his discussion of cases when civilized nations could use force for reasons not related to security and the common law of self-defense.[224]. Mill's article, in addressing these three purposes against the backdrop of the diplomatic politics over the

Suez Canal project provides three aspects worth discussing in light of the imperial democratization and good governance theorem that he gives in *Considerations*.

The first aspect is Mill's English exceptionalism. By this I mean his general view that England is the most "civilized" and "advanced" nation in the modern world of his day, which he believes the hopes of humanity depend upon.[225] In sum, Mill presents England as a special nation with a special character in a special moment in history.[226] The second major aspect is Mill's civilizational language. In this article Mill not only divides humanity into the civilized and non-civilized theorizing how the conduct of each should be in their relations, but Mill also employs his conception of civilization and his ideal of civilizational progress in a practical context, the French pursuit of the Suez Canal project. Finally, Mill's combination of imperialism and democratization is advocated in his discussion of cases beyond the common right of self-defense when civilized nations can use force through intervention.[227] I will outline each of these two aspects before discussing Mill's much earlier essay "Civilization" (1836).

Mill's English exceptionalism is the first substantive point of "A Few Words on Non-Intervention." Mill writes that of all the nations in the world it is only England whose "declared principle" of foreign policy is "to let other nations alone" even though England is "equal to the greatest in extent of dominion" and "far exceeding any other" in wealth and "in power that wealth bestows."[228] Mill elaborates the point writing that any attempt England "makes to exert influence" over others "even by persuasion" is "rather in the service of others than of itself."[229] Mill writes that the English nation with its non-meddling foreign policy is such a "novelty in the world" that its continental critics are unable to recognize its selfless principles which are for "the benefit of all mankind."[230]

Mill illustrates this in his argument that England when it defeats a "barbarian" nation in war allows it to "command liberty in trade;" for Mill what England "demands for itself it demands for the benefit of all mankind."[231]

Another explicit assertion of Mill's English exceptionalism in the article is in his claim that the English people:

> are now in one of those critical moments, which do not occur once in a generation, when the whole turn of European events, and the course of European history for a long time to come, may depend on the conduct and on the estimation of England.[232]

One can interpret this passage in the context of this article in three ways. First, it can be interpreted as a broad statement meant to support Mill's general view of England's historic position in late modernity as the most civilized and advanced nation. Second, it can be interpreted as a statement meant to support the distinction Mill makes between the character of English people versus the blunders of the then English politicians (namely the Prime Minister). Or, most narrowly, it can be interpreted as a statement to support his view of what the English government ought to do regarding the French claim to the Suez Canal project. My own view is that for Mill it fits and supports all three of these general and related validity claims which I take Mill to hold. Possible debate over these various interpretations need not be resolved here because any of these possible interpretations or any combination thereof involves Mill's English exceptionalism in which England is a special nation with a special character in a special moment in history.

For Mill, England is "incomparably the most conscientious of all nations." Mill elaborates this point writing that among nations which "are sufficiently powerful to be capable of being dangerous to its neighbours" England is perhaps "the only one whom mere scruples of conscience would suffice to deter" the English from using this capability.[233]

Regarding the second major aspect, Mill's civilizational language, Mill applies his concept of "civilization" to his analysis of the Suez Canal project. Recall that Mill's concept of civilization includes material development as well as moral development. Also recall that Mill is interested in the relationship between these two forms of civilization because material development is necessary for moral development, but too much or too little material development can be an obstacle to moral development and therefore to civilizational progress. In light of this concept of civilization and of Mill's emphasis on the relationship between moral and material development, we see Mill endorse the idea of the French attempt to carry forward the Suez Canal project based on this notion of civilization with an eye to civilizational progress when he writes:

> this scheme, if realized, will save, on one of the great highways of the world's traffic, the circumnavigation of a continent. An easy access of commerce is the main source of that material civilization, which, in the more backward regions of the earth, is the necessary condition and indispensable machinery of the moral; and this scheme reduces practically by one half, the distance, commercially speaking, between the self-improving. The Atlantic Telegraph is esteemed an enterprise of world-wide importance because it abridges the transit of mercantile intelligence merely. What the Suez Canal would shorten is the transport of the goods themselves, and this to such an extent as probably to augment it manifold.[234]

Mill's division of humanity into the civilized and non-civilized is also entailed in the passage above but is elaborated even more extensively in the aspect of his article that deals with the use of military force and imperial democratization.

The last part of Mill's article identifies the need for rational criteria to determine when nations can use force to intervene in the affairs of other nations. Mill's first move in this is to distinguish the doctrine of non-intervention as it applies to the conduct between civilized nations versus the way it applies to the conduct between civilized nations and non-civilized nations. Here Mill also refers to the "non-civilized" as "barbarian neighbours" and nations with "a lesser degree of civilization."[235] Mill couples this division with a strong statement of his imperial democratization ideas for having superior nations rule and therefore improve inferior nations. Mill writes thus:

> To suppose that the same international customs, and the same rules of international morality, can obtain between one civilized nation and another, and between civilized nations and barbarians, is a grave error....In the first place, the rules of ordinary international morality imply reciprocity. But barbarians will not reciprocate. They cannot be depended on for observing rules. Their minds are not capable of so great an effort....In the next place, nations which are still barbarous have not got beyond the period during which it is likely to be their benefit that they should be conquered and held into subjection by foreigners. Independence and nationality, so essential to the due growth and development of a people further advanced in improvement, are generally impediments to theirs. The sacred duties which civilized nations owe to the independence and nationality of each other, are not binding towards those to whom nationality and independence are either a certain evil, or at best a questionable good.[236]

Mill backs up this civilizational division and imperial democratization prescription in no uncertain terms adding that:

> To characterize any conduct whatever towards a barbarous people as a violation of the law of nations, only shows that he who speaks has never considered the subject. A violation of great principles of morality it may easily be; but barbarians have no rights as a *nation,* except a right to such treatment as may, at the earliest possible period, fit them for becoming one.[237]

Immediately following these illuminating passages Mill goes into a defense of British rule of India and French rule of Algeria, most extensively regarding the former on the basis that it improves barbarous neighbors through the use of force by ending the barbarous communities native despotism and by providing them with good governance through the good despotism of foreign rule.[238] Mill does also discuss the "unhappy"

British history of poor foreign rule but sees the rule of the British East India Company in his day as outside of this history.[239] Mill ends the article by discussing cases where nations are justified in intervening with military force beyond those situations covered under the auspices of security and the common law of self-defense.[240] Mill's discussion of these cases is noteworthy for two reasons.

One reason is that we see an early use of Mill's will and ability clause which is the core of his first chapter of *Considerations* and a primary component of the architecture of his theorem. I also outline Mill's three test cases when intervention is permissible beyond self-defense to illustrate the application of Mill's will and ability clause, which in a series of three conditions holds that peoples must be ready, willing and able to protect and operate the form of government in question. And, finally, I outline these cases to illustrate Mill's endorsement of imperial rule for the improvement of other nations for the ends of civilizational progress. I turn to these cases now.

(1) Mill thinks intervention to assist other governments against their own population is often not justifiable because a "government which needs foreign support to enforce obedience from its own citizens, is one which ought not to exist."[241]

(2) In the case of protracted civil war with no near end to be rationally deduced, or the probable end is that of the victorious side enforcing repugnant governance which is "injurious to the permanent welfare of the country," Mill thinks neighbouring countries or "one powerful country with the acquiescence of the rest" are entitled to intervene to end the conflict and enforce terms of reconciliation.[242]

(3) The third case is on "whether a country is justified in helping the people of another in a struggle against their own government for free institutions".[243] Mill thinks the answer

depends on whether the government that natives are resisting is of a "purely native government" or not.[244] Regarding the former Mill says intervention is not justified since the "only test possessing any real value" of a people "becoming fit for popular institutions." is that a sufficient portion of them "are willing to brave labour and danger" for "their liberation."[245] Regarding the case of native resistance to foreign government or a native tyranny upheld by foreign arms, Mill thinks intervention is justified because the native resistors by resisting this despotic rule are displaying a will for freedom, therefore satisfying the first condition of the will and ability clause.[246] Because the people possess this will they should not have been interfered with by the more powerful nation. In other words when a more powerful intervener violates the doctrine of non-intervention by acting against another nation in a way that hinders their civilizational progress, the original intervener has created a circumstance in which intervention by other nations is justified to correct this injustice. Mill says here that

> intervention to enforce non-intervention is always rightful, always moral, if not always prudent. Though it be a mistake to *give* freedom to a people who do not value the boon, it cannot be right to insist that if they do value it, they shall be hindered from the pursuit of it by foreign occupation.[247]

I have used "A Few Words on Non-Intervention" to further illustrate, against the practical backdrop of the 1859 international politics over the Suez Canal project, Mill's English exceptionalism, Mill's use of his notion of civilization, and Mill's imperial democratization ideas for the ends of civilizational progress. I now turn to Mill's early essay "Civilization" (1836) which is Mill's extensive essay on the notion of civilization to further examine Mill's meaning of this important term.

"Civilization": "A Word with Double Meaning"

Mill's essay "Civilization," which precedes *Considerations* by 25 years, entails his most explicit focus on the meaning of civilization. In addition to adding to my explication of Mill's imperial democratization theorem it is important for any scholar on Mill and imperialism to give careful attention to this text because the different patterns of interpretations and normative postures that distinguish the critical literature from the sympathetic, pivot around contestation over Mill's meaning of civilization particularly based on readings of this text. My examination of this text here is an important part of my account of how the sympathetic literature misuses this text to problematize the portrayal of Mill in critical literature. The sympathetic literature is the subject of my final chapter.

Mill begins the text by stating that civilization is a word with "double meaning."[248] For Mill "it sometimes stands for human improvement in general" and sometimes for "human improvement in particular."[249] Note here how Mill is not saying that civilization is a word with two separate meanings but rather like many "other terms in philosophy of human nature" civilization has a general meaning and a particular meaning. As I show in my explication of Mill below, I take Mill to mean that the term has two related elements, a general normative sense and a particular descriptive sense. As I discuss in the following chapter this is not how the sympathetic literature understands this essay which is why, I argue, their critiques of critical literature and their understanding of Mill's imperialism are erroneous and a distorted portrayal of these works in question.

Regarding the general meaning Mill, says "we are more accustomed to call a country civilized if we think it more improved," that is "more eminent in the best characteristics of Man and Society," and further advanced "in the road to perfection; happier, nobler, wiser."[250] I refer to this broader meaning as moral development. Regarding human improvement in the particular, Mill says that the term civilization "stands for that kind of improvement only, which distinguishes a wealthy and powerful nation from savages or barbarians." I refer to this narrow meaning as material development.[251]

Mill then states that this essay aims to examine the narrow meaning of the term, material development, for two reasons. One reason is that Mill sees his present era of human history as "the era of civilization in this narrow sense" and so an inquiry into material development is "calculated to throw light upon the many characteristic features of our time."[252] A second reason is that Mill sees an important question in that "we entertain no doubt" that narrow civilization "is a good" yet we "may speak of the vices or the miseries" of it.[253] Mill is interested in examining the tension between these two features of the narrow meaning of civilization as they relate to the broader normative sense of civilizational improvement.

There are three aspects of this text which I will outline below. First is that Mill is examining material development to figure out how to reap the benefits of this type of "civilizational advancement" for "broader civilizational progress"[254] which for Mill necessarily includes both material and moral development. Second, following from Mill's understanding of this problem is the pedagogical framework of some of Mill's ideas for addressing the problem and promoting civilizational progress.[255] Third is that Mill links his ideas for pedagogical correction of the harms of narrow civilization, intended to reap material development's contributions to civilizational progress, to ideas on the proper forms of political and democratic organization for the ends of civilizational progress.

Regarding the first, Mill describes the effects of material improvement which have occurred most eminently in degree and in "more rapid progression" in Great Britain. The mega consequence for Mill here is the weakening of the power of the few and an increase in the power of the many; the transfer of power from a few highly cultivated individuals to a mediocre many constituting a mass. Material improvement does this because it redistributes the extensive property holdings and the intellectual abilities held by the few in aristocratic circles into smaller parcels belonging to a mass constituted by an emerging middle class that did not exist prior to rapid material development.[256] Mill considers this shift in power to be the political effects of material development on humankind.

Mill then outlines two types of moral consequences of material development: the direct influence of material development on individual character and "the moral effects produced by the insignificance into which the individual falls in comparison with the masses."[257] Mill theorizes that the former causes the character of the individual to relax in individual energy, to concentrate in "the narrow sphere of the individual's money-getting pursuits," and to become "dependent on what most nearly concerns him," relying "not upon his own exertions" but upon the "general arrangements of society" such as "his family" and "property."[258]

On the insignificance of the individual in relation to mass, Mill sees the problem to be that in countries with extensive material development those of higher class are nearly extinct as their potential nobility is reshaped by mass; in other words the power of mass replaces higher pursuits by valuing monetary pursuits only.[259] The higher class individuals and their more noble endeavors are crowded out by the power of mass, meaning the influence of the more cultivated few is weakened and the influence of the less cultivated majority is strengthened.[260] Mill frames this as the creation of a cowardly

passive opulent class and the destruction of an active heroic class which in turn results in

the corruption of "the very fountain of improvement of public opinion itself.[261]

The above is Mill's understanding of the problem of the harms of material

development on moral development which he thinks will "continue until met by some

system of cultivation adopted to counteract it."[262] The tension is that although Mill thinks

material development is "without doubt... assuredly" a good,[263] material development

has both beneficial and harmful tendencies. That Mill is concerned in this essay with this

problem and therefore the role of both meanings of "civilization" in civilizational

progress is clear and apparent when Mill writes:

> Is there, then, no remedy? Are the decay of individual energy, the weakening of
> the influence of superior minds over the multitude, the growth of *charlatanerie*,
> and the diminished efficacy of public opinion as a restraining power,—are these
> the price we necessarily pay for the benefits of civilization; and can they only be
> avoided by checking the diffusion of knowledge, discouraging the spirit of
> combination, prohibiting improvements in the arts of life, and repressing the
> further increase of wealth and of production? Assuredly not. Those advantages
> which civilization cannot give—which in its uncorrected influence it has even a
> tendency to destroy—may yet coexist with civilization; and it is only when joined
> to civilization that they can produce their fairest fruits. All that we are in danger
> of losing we may preserve, all that we have lost we may regain, and bring to a
> perfection hitherto unknown; but not by slumbering, and leaving things to
> themselves, no more than by ridiculously trying our strength against their
> irresistible tendencies: only be establishing counter-tendencies, which may
> combine with those tendencies, and modify them.[264]

Mill's ideas for counteracting the second type of harmful tendencies, the loss of

cultivated individuality to the mediocrity of the masses, are "national institutions of

education, and forms of polity," that are "calculated to invigorate the individual

character."[265] The notion of forms of polity to "gradually train" and "discipline people"

through "practices" to acquire the necessary character for civilizational progress that Mill provides in this essay constitutes a small gesture towards the sophisticated theorem Mill publishes in *Considerations* 25 years later. In "Civilization" Mill theorizes how national institutions of university education can produce intellectuals with the proper character to hold positions of an MP or an editor of London newspapers; Mill cites the two positions as the only occupation an individual can hold to satisfy their noble character and counteract the harmful tendencies of material development while defending its benefits. Mill saw himself playing this noble role of cultivated intellectual educating the public by holding these positions himself during his own life.

In sum, I have illustrated that in "Civilization" Mill thinks of civilizational progress as containing both the narrow sense of the term and the broad sense of the term, both material advancement and moral advancement with the relationship between these elements being a crucial concern for his particular understanding of civilizational progress which form the normative axis of Mill's thought. As we will see in the following chapter, however, the sympathetic literature does not account for all of these aspects of Mill's essay. And therefore, sympathetic literature brings an erroneous interpretation of civilizational progress into its critique of the critical literature and, moreover, provides an overarching and extensively problematic rendering of Mill and imperialism.

Chapter 3

Sympathetic Standpoints

This chapter turns to three recent works on Mill that I group together as sympathetic standpoints. Recall that I call sympathetic standpoints those works on Mill that argue against the framing of Mill as imperialist, or, that argue that Mill's imperialism is a just and tolerant theory of imperialism that should be applied to issues in global politics. There are three broad purposes to this chapter. One is to respond to the objections to my standpoint on Mill and imperialism that are inherent in this literature. Second is to review and assess this literature as genuine scholarship on Mill and imperialism. Third is to identify a growing need for critical engagement with this sympathetic literature which has only emerged in the last two years. Ultimately I argue against the portrait of Mill that this literature provides because I hold that Mill is imperialist and that his political vision, especially his imperial democratization and good governance theorem, should not be applied in the contemporary world.

The three articles I group as sympathetic standpoints are the following listed, in the order in which each is discussed. The first is "A Tale of Two Indias: Burke and Mill on Empire and Slavery in the West Indies and America" (2006).[266] This article argues against critical literature and posits that Mill should not be simply understood as an imperialist. The second is "Tolerant Imperialism: John Stuart Mill's Defense of British Rule in India" (2006).[267] And the third is "Intervention and Empire: John Stuart Mill and International Relations" (2005).[268] These latter two articles are different than the first in that they argue that Mill's imperialism is a form of imperialism that is applicable to classic and contemporary global issues.

Kohn and O'Neill: Mill and the West Indies

In their 2006 article "A Tale of Two Indias: Burke and Mill on Empire and Slavery in the West Indies and America" Margaret Kohn and Daniel O'Neill provide a sympathetic standpoint on Mill's relationship to imperialism.[269] The larger purpose for the authors is to challenge the "new scholarly orthodoxy surrounding Edmund Burke's and JS Mill's views of the imperial project."[270] Kohn and O'Neill, referring to the work of Uday Mehta

and Jennifer Pitts, sum up this new orthodoxy noting how such scholarship portrays Mill

as "attempting to synthesize historical progressivism" to "justify benign despotism" as a

means "to foster good government" and "the development of individual rationality" in

contrast to their view of Burke.[271] The interpretation of Burke in this new orthodoxy is as

"a defender of cultural pluralism and difference."[272] Their method for challenging this

new orthodoxy is to rethink Burke's and Mill's relationship to imperialism through their

political actions and writings on the West Indies as opposed to their work on India.[273]

Burke's and Mill's work on India grounds the scholarship of Mehta and Pitts who form

this new orthodoxy.

Kohn and O'Neill argue that Burke's and Mill's respective positions on the West

Indies complicate the portrayal of these thinkers by the new orthodoxy because a

comparison of these positions point to a contrary conclusion, emphasizing Burke as a

more committed British imperialist than Mill.[274] Kohn and O'Neill go so far as to claim

that such a comparison complicates portraying Mill as a committed British imperialist in

general. They provide an excellent scholarly contribution in soundly challenging the

portrait of Burke provided in the works by Mehta and Pitts. But Burke aside, Kohn and

O'Neill's sympathetic standpoint on Mill does not hold based on the analysis they

provide on Mill. My position is that although the new scholarly orthodoxy incorrectly

holds that Burke is not imperialist, as shown by Kohn and O'Neill, it rightly argues that

Mill is extensively imperialist. In other words Kohn and O'Neill, in contrast to the new

orthodoxy, incorrectly hold that Mill is less imperialist than Burke even though they

correctly identify Burke's relationship to imperialism.

In sum, my view is different than both perspectives because unlike the new scholarly orthodoxy and unlike Kohn and O'Neill I view both Burke and Mill as promoting imperialism in their political works and contexts. I am more concerned with Mill because it is he that designs an imperial democratization and good governance theorem to guide policy for actually civilizing others towards an English model of governance for the ends of civilizational progress. Burke is beyond the scope of this thesis so I will limit myself to a review and assessment of Kohn's and O'Neill's portrayal of Mill.

They claim that casting Mill as "the leading proponent of empire" is "misleading."[275] To support their claim they point first to Mill's political actions and writings on the West Indies and Jamaica. Second they point to what they view as a misunderstanding of Mill's concept of civilization in the new orthodoxy's framing of Mill as an imperialist. Below I examine both bases of Kohn's and O'Neill's standpoint.

The first basis has two components and I outline each here. First, Mill "jeopardized his parliamentary career by publicly prosecuting a colonial governor for injustice and cruelty committed in the colonies."[276] Kohn and O'Neill portray Mill as "recognizing the legitimacy of anti-imperialist sentiment" by outlining the way he sacrificed his seat in the British House of Commons to lead a group of British citizens in pursuing the prosecution of a former governor of Jamaica who committed a number of atrocities against Black colonial subjects.[277] Coupled with this sacrifice, Kohn and O'Neill see Mill's anti-imperialist moment in these events as apparent when he explained to his electors that he had "felt called upon to protest 'against a precedent that could justly inflame against us the people of our dependencies'"[278] and also in that Mill carried out highly visible criticism of "English brutality in Jamaica between 1865-1867."[279] 2) Second, Kohn and

O'Neill note that Mill argued for "black emancipation" in the West Indies in his article "The Negro Question."[280]

These two components, as Kohn and O'Neill themselves acknowledge, do not "seriously disturb the portrait of Mill we have from his writings on India."[281] Furthermore, it is problematic that Kohn and O'Neill take Mill's use of the qualifier "justly" as a significant implication that he "recognized the legitimacy of an anti-imperialist sentiment" without more thoroughly considering the role imperialism plays in Mill's theory of just relations between civilized ruler and their non-civilized dependencies.[282] As I illustrated in the first two chapters of my thesis and as is recognized explicitly in the two additional sympathetic standpoints I discuss below, for Mill justice is not mutually exclusive from imperialism but rather imperialism and justice should often go together. By noting that these two components are not sufficient to complicate the imperial representation of Mill we get from his writings on India Kohn and O'Neill belie their central claim. This claim was that pointing towards Mill's position on the West Indies would constitute a complication of the imperial representation of Mill we get from his writings on India.

Regarding Mill's use of the term "civilization," Kohn and O'Neill posit that Mill's conception of civilization is misunderstood as a hierarchical and normative concept in critical standpoints that frame Mill as a proponent of imperialism when in fact it is a narrow descriptive term referring to economic development.[283] Kohn and O'Neill base this critique on their particular use of Mill's article "Civilization" which is not a work specific to the West Indies. They note that one has to understand that Mill's category of civilization, which he inherited from Scottish Enlightenment historiography, only connotes Mill's narrower sense of the term referring to economic development, what I labeled following Beate Jahn as material development.[284] Secondly they argue that scholars who portray Mill as endorsing despotic rule of barbarians by the civilized misunderstand Mill's position because they misunderstand the meaning and scope of his category of civilization by viewing it as the broader normative category which includes ethnocentric and racial hierarchies rather than the narrower descriptive economic category.[285] In addition to this they cite Mill's critique and fear of civilization in the narrow sense (economic development) as crowding out high culture and individuality, as proof of his explicit rejection of the position that civilization always leads to progress, promoting progress for humanity being Mill's ultimate concern and project.[286]

As is clear from my discussion of Mill's essay "Civilization," I think Kohn and O'Neill are correct to look to "Civilization" to reflect on Mill's wielding of the term "civilization" and are also correct in noting that Mill has two meanings of the term, a broad normative meaning and a narrow descriptive meaning as Mill stipulates at the beginning of the essay. That said, however, Kohn and O'Neill fail to explicate the way in which Mill sees material civilization as necessary, even if not always sufficient nor beneficial, for civilizational progress. And related to the latter point, Kohn and O'Neill fail to explicate the way in which Mill is concerned with formulating this relationship in a way that best promotes civilizational progress which for Mill necessarily includes both material and moral improvement, or in the terms Kohn and O'Neill employ, both broad normative improvement and narrow descriptive improvement.

Indeed one of the important purposes of Mill's imperialism, including his imperial democratization theorem, is to reap the benefits of material development while correcting for its harmful effects. It is the relationship between material development and moral development for the ends of civilizational progress in normatively heavy connotations of the term that is significant to Mill in this essay. This relationship is clearly one that Mill is intensely concerned with throughout his writings but specifically in "Civilization" because he thinks this relationship is crucial to the civilizational progress that Mill values more than anything. Civilizational progress is the normative axis of Mill's political vision in "Civilization" as elsewhere which is why the second half the article is all about education, because Mill believes that the proper training of elite intellectuals can correct for the harms of material development while enabling society to reap its benefits.[287]

Because Kohn and O'Neill fail to recognize the significance of this relationship between the two meanings of civilization in Mill's more comprehensive notion of civilization they are guilty of the error they claim Mehta and Pitts make.[288] Compared to the critical standpoint authors, it is Kohn and O'Neill who actually most misunderstand Mill's civilizational language. Moreover, because of Kohn and O'Neill's misunderstanding of Mill's civilizational language and perhaps also because they, like all Mill scholars to date, have not confronted any scholarly research that identifies and focuses on Mill's imperial democratization theorem they fail to incorporate the small but noteworthy gesture towards this theorem that exists in "Civilization." In sum, Kohn and O'Neill fail to realize the fit between Mill's essay "Civilization" and Mill's imperialism.

Ultimately Kohn and O'Neill conclude that Mill cannot simply be reduced in our understandings to being a committed British imperialist and that his various writings and actions cannot be coherently reconciled under such a portrayal.[289] But I have illustrated above why this sympathetic standpoint on Mill is problematic; Kohn and O'Neill have not actually provided an account that prevents a coherent reconciliation of Mill as a committed British imperialist. If anything, all that Kohn and O'Neill show persuasively is that Mill's thought holds that British imperialism should operate in a specific way along particular guidelines that adhere to specific conduct, what the other sympathetic standpoints frame as just imperialism and what I argue is the purpose of the imperial democratization theorem outlined in *Considerations*. But it is important to note that this broad fact, that Mill has a modular form of imperialism, is consistent with and supports the standpoint on Mill I provide in the first two chapters of this thesis. But I, unlike the next two sympathetic standpoints I discuss below, do not think Mill's modular form of imperialism is actually good and applicable, in fact and theory, to contemporary issues.

Mark Tunick: Mill and Tolerant Imperialism

Like Kohn and O'Neill Mark Tunick challenges the portrayal of Mill in critical standpoint literature in his article "Tolerant Imperialism: John Stuart Mill's Defense of British Rule in India" (2006).[290] Tunick argues that Mill does not advocate imperialism that seeks to forcefully intervene with the non-civilized to reshape their way of being.[291] Instead, according to Tunick, Mill advocates a tolerant imperialism applied to the civilized and non-civilized alike that respects other ways of being by imposing the proper legal, social and political institutions that are required to protect diversity and plurality.[292] In concluding his article Tunick provides his view of Mill's tolerant imperialism and its relevance to the contemporary world, writing:

> The issue we should address with Mill in mind is whether it is a good idea to interfere in the affairs of other states in order to promote legal rights, respect, and toleration for conflicting viewpoints and ways of life, and a commercial society that can cope with natural threats, given that such interference may threaten the hegemony of existing forms of life in which people have deeply invested identities but perhaps fewer alternatives, rather than the issue—false

where Mill is concerned—of whether the West should forcibly reshape the rest of the world in its own image.[293]

In this gesture towards the application of Mill's tolerant imperialism in the contemporary world Tunick's rhetoric avoids the mixed connotations of imperialism altogether mentioning only the less accurate but also less politicized term interference.

There are three parts to my review and assessment of Tunick's standpoint on Mill and imperialism. First I outline his critique of critical authors such as Bhikhu Parekh and Uday Mehta. Second I will further explicate Tunick's understanding of Mill's tolerant imperialism. Third I critique Tunick's presentation of Mill as a tolerant imperialist. Regarding the third part, I particularly critique Tunick's distinction between tolerant imperialism and intolerant imperialism.

Before getting into each of these parts it is necessary to note three things. First is that Tunick thinks Mill's imperialism is difficult to interpret correctly because of the tension between some of Mill's fundamental concepts which today are assumed to be non-commensurable.[294] These are the notions of liberty, toleration, and imperialism.[295] Second is that Tunick thinks that although many presume that tolerance and imperialism are incommensurable, if by imperialism we merely mean any type of interference or imposition to some possible end and not necessarily ends that are self-interested, overtly violent, or aiming to normatively reshape others in the imperializer's own image, then tolerance and imperialism can and do go together.[296] It is by narrowing his meaning of imperialism to mean only what has just been described above that Tunick frames Mill's imperialism as not a necessarily a bad thing.[297] Third, and related to the second, is that since Tunick interprets Mill's imperialism to be not self-interested, not advocating the application of hard overt violence and physical force, and not aiming to normatively reorder other ways of being, he thinks Mill does achieve a tolerant imperialism.[298]

Tunick understands the critical scholarship as framing Mill as an "undisputed spokesperson for British imperialism" viewing England and the East India Company as "forces of progress that spread values and improve mankind's capacity for individuality."[299] Tunick interprets Parekh as incorrectly holding that Mill advocates despotism for non-Western people to destroy their non-liberal ways of life and Methta as incorrectly viewing Mill as articulating a cosmopolitan "dictatorship of reason" that homogenizes others in encounters with unfamiliar cultural difference.[300] There are two main bases of Tunick's critique. One is that he views Parekh and Mehta as misunderstanding Mill's meaning of "civilization," a second is that Tunick claims that Parekh and Mehta misrepresent Mill's position on the application of tolerant imperialism in India in four ways.

Regarding the first, Tunick thinks that Parekh and Mehta have improperly reconciled tensions in Mill's thought by arguing that he has two different standards, one for the civilized and one for the non-civilized.[301] Tunick argues that Mill actually holds the civilized and the non-civilized to the same standard; his tolerant imperialism applies internally and externally.[302] Furthermore, Tunick thinks that Parekh and Mehta have misunderstood the meaning of civilization along the same lines as what was outlined in my discussion of Kohn and O'Neill above.[303] There is no need for me reproduce my view of Mill's civilizational language and a critique of Kohn and O'Neill's problematization of the critical understandings of this language here; merely note that this same view and critique apply here.

Regarding the second, Tunick argues that between Parekh and Mehta, there are four misrepresentations of Mill's position on the use of tolerant imperialism in the British rule of India. One is that Mill's tolerant imperialism does not entail assimilation.[304] Second is that Mill's despotism does not deny the rights of those it governs nor uses power against Indians arbitrarily.[305] Third is that Mill tolerates even illiberal practices of Indians and recognizes the importance of such in their lives.[306] Fourth is that even though Mill imposes limits on his tolerance of practices, these are not based on racist or ethnocentric views of difference as asserted by Parekh and Mehta, but are based on a tension between liberty and moral development both of which Mill was committed to.[307] Tunick notes that Mill's limits on tolerance through the no-harm principle apply to both the civilized and the non-civilized.

Tunick provides a plethora of examples to support his charge of these four misrepresentations which he thinks are based on a misrecognition that although Mill "thinks some harmful practices outside the bounds of reason should be abolished" he is committed to a policy of accommodation and recommends a "gentle means of reform" for even the harmful practices.[308] Tunick distinguishes this from Mill's personal attitudes of intolerance as seen in his representation and personal criticisms of "embarrassing practices" in the "little-advanced civilization" of India in letters to Coleridge and Comte regarding infanticide, sati, witchcraft, and tragga.[309]

The examples Tunick cites from Mill's professional and political career are the following. One is that Mill endorsed a freedom of religion policy in an 1858 petition, supporting the continuation of the East India Company's rule of India, advocating that it is right "to abstain from banning religious practices except those that are abhorrent."[310]

Second is Mill's recommendation for the non-abolishment of reasonable practices such as those of banditry and bahirwattia. Third is Mill's 1837 recommendation to replace the deceased king of Oudh with a local heir rather than annexation and amalgamation with surrounding states.[311] Fourth is Mill's supposed divergence from Lord Thomas Macaulay's view that education policy should be geared to creating a "class who may be interpreters between us and the millions whom we govern; a class of persons, Indian in blood and colour but English in taste, in opinions, in morals, and in intellect" by providing an Anglican education in India rather than an Orientalist education as some of Mill's and Macaulay's contemporaries consistently advocated.

In brief response to Tunick's account it should be noted that these examples of tolerance and accommodation do not problematize the views on Mill held by Mehta and Parekh. Rather they fit with Parekh's reading of Mill that inferior peoples are subjected to the judgment of superior peoples' narrow notion of diversity and reason.[312] This account also fits Mehta's view that in liberalism's relationship to empire, modular and particular notions of reason were developed first in the local contexts of Europe and were then applied universally to the unfamiliar others Europe encountered in the historical experience of colonialism and imperialism, thereby homogenizing them through force.[313] Furthermore, Tunick's account also does not problematize my identification and explication of Mill's imperial democratization and good governance theorem because these examples of tolerance provided by Tunick show John Stuart Mill's theorem in action, the gradual training of others through multiple stages towards the reasonable way of being.

At the core of Tunick's understanding of Mill's tolerant imperialism is the distinction between tolerant imperialism and intolerant imperialism by which Tunick constructs a dualistic typology. The former, according to Tunick, forces modular Western institutions on the civilized and the non-civilized alike to protect values of agency, choice, diversity, plurality, and security; in other words to enforce tolerance itself.[314] Distinct from this tolerant imperialism, intolerant imperialisms are types of imperialism carried-out for self-interest, advocate overt violence, and seek to reshape the non-civilized towards a Western way of being against values of choice, agency, diversity, and plurality and breeching the security of the imperialized to be free from dangerous and threatening imperial intervention and interference.[315] The distinction being noted, I do not see how the version of tolerant imperialism that Tunick abstracts from Mill is mutually exclusive from the types of imperialism that he frames as intolerant and irrelevant to discussions on Mill. Tunick's dualistic typology is a false dichotomy both in general and in relation to Mill's imperialism.

Ultimately the practices of tolerant imperialism as understood by Tunick, the upholding of rights, the non-use of arbitrary power, the tolerance of illiberal practices, and the lack of ethnocentrism[316] are presented in a superficial and distorted manner. For example, the rights upheld, even if some of these are locally held practices, are selected by the "superior" peoples. Moreover, the meaning of arbitrariness in relation to the use of disciplinary power is defined by the "superior" peoples. Furthermore, the reasonableness of practices is judged by "superior" peoples. The paradigms Mill uses to distinguish these subjective qualities, such as "reasonableness" and "arbitrariness" is civilizational progress which is assessed against an ethnocentric civilizational standard in which most of humanity is unreasonably "barbaric" and therefore require despotic force from superior peoples. This is what necessarily goes into imposing Tunick's Millian inspired modular form of the proper legal, social, political order on the non-civilized and in imposing Millian system of governance that works along these lines. This brings into question, and in my view completely reveals, the lack of substance in Tunick's distinction between tolerant imperialism and intolerant imperialism, especially when Mill is held up as an exemplary icon of the former.

Tunick never engages with the fact that Mill's meaning and view of representative government as the best constitution for humanity is a European, most specifically English, form of government, and that to impose this system and its earlier intermediacies on others through foreign rule, even if truly benevolent in intent, implies and involves the threat and the use of violence. And, contrary to Tunick's portrayal, for Mill the means of imposing representative government as the right political, social, and legal constitutional order involves the premise that other ways of being should be reshaped in ways to fit with the conduct necessary for the form of government in question.[317] These points are clearly illustrated in my explication of *Considerations* in the previous chapter which, in conjunction with the entirety of chapters one and two, clearly illustrates how Mill's imperialism, contra Tunick, involves both force and the reshaping of a plurality of others towards an English way of being.

Carol Prager: Realism, Prudence, and the Acuity of Mill's Imperialism

Carol Prager provides another sympathetic reading of Mill in her article "Intervention and Empire: John Stuart Mill and International Relations" (2005). Carol Prager examines Mill's relationship to intervention and empire because she is puzzled by the lack of attention given to Mill in IR scholarship, especially in the English School which Prager notes has a tradition of paying "special attention to the contributions of classical political philosophers to international discourse."[318] Prager finds Mill's work "practical for statesmen" and valuable for thinking through contemporary issues because Mill "identified timeless problems intrinsic to IR" while appreciating the tensions that existed in principles behind courses of action, the requirements of circumstances, and the probability of unintended consequences.[319] Prager explicates that Mill's combination of personal life struggles, romantic individualism, utilitarian ethics and his public and professional engagement with the classic problems of intervention and empire in international affairs are all elements of what makes Mill a "realistic" and "prudent" thinker. Mill, Prager thinks, should be praised for his "acuity" of vision regarding questions of imperialism rather than represented as "a fervent supporter of empire."[320]

To outline Prager's portrayal of Mill I will first go through an account of a number of aspects of Mill's imperialism that are discussed by Prager. I start with Prager's account of Mill's understanding of intervention and interference and how they relate to Mill's civilizational language. Then I provide Prager's view of Mill's meaning of "barbarous". After this I turn to Prager's account of the way that Mill's concept of nationality parallels his concept of individuality. Finally, I outline Prager's account of Mill's ideas on intervention and empire particularly regarding Mill's prudent limitations on foreign rule and intervention. Secondly, I discuss Prager's contrast between the acuity and prudence of Mill's limited imperial intervention versus the idealism of contemporary cosmopolitanism with its much bolder willingness to employ intervention in non-Western states.

Prager argues that Mill "arrived at an understanding of intervention and interference that he elaborated in the contexts" of civilized and barbarous "states."[321] By intervention Prager means "overt intrusion to achieve a specific" limited object and by interference she means more "far-reaching, penetrating involvement, including empire and what we call today nation-building."[322] Prager adds that Mill believed that interference in civilized states "was generally unjustified" and intervention as Prager uses the term "rarely sufficed" for Mill in regards to barbarous and semi-barbarous ones. Prager does not examine the civilizational language in depth but asserts that what Mill means by barbarous was "intuitively obvious to him" and that Mill sets up a civilizational continuum from primitive to civilized that parallels a continuum that runs from intervention to interference.[323] Finally, it is worth noting that Prager emphasizes that for Mill questions of intervention were things to be judged on moral considerations in light of circumstances rather than to be judged on legal ones.[324]

On Mill's meaning of nationality, Prager notes that Mill had a concept of nationality that was distinct from a concept of ethnicity. This is seen by the fact that, for Mill, civilized countries "had a high degree of nationality" whereas the non-civilized "had little or none."[325] Prager, notes moreover, that for Mill "a strong and active principle of nationality" was an "essential condition which has existed in all durable societies.[326] Prager elaborates on the similarities between Mill's notion of nationality and Mill's notion of individuality as they relate to imperial intervention. Prager writes thus:

> The counterpart to individuality, full-blown nationality, provided the rationale for ruling out intervention. A people displaying true nationality, in contrast with semi-barbarous and barbarous people, were entitled to be free from intervention. The autonomy that was underwritten by nationality took the form of national self-determination, and it was this process to which outsiders were obliged to defer.[327]

On Mill's views on empire and intervention Prager, contrary to my account, reads "A Few Words of Non-Intervention" as an article where Mill's "prudence reigned supreme" because he supported a doctrine of non-intervention with only four exceptional cases. Recall that I read this article as aspects of Mill's imperial democratization theorem being applied in the politics surrounding the Suez Canal. Like Mark Tunick, Prager also argues that Mill was "not intellectually a wholehearted supporter of empire" because in his working life with the East India Company he "tended to favour restraint in interference" in local Indian affairs. Also like Tunick, Prager finds further reason in this claim in that Mill thought that "imperial rule 'was the highest moral trust which can devolve upon a nation'" and in his view that Britain's obligations were not exhausted by satisfying its self-interest.[328]

Another reason for Prager's position here, which is also cited in Tunick's sympathetic standpoint, is Mill's support for his employers' continued rule of India on the basis that as a foreign ruler the East India Company "shielded India from any crass British political interest."[329] Prager sees Mill's concerns with these issues as being exemplified by the fact that Mill claimed that "it has been the destiny of the government of the East India Company, to suggest the true theory of government of a semi-barbarous dependency of a civilized country."[330] In further support of this sympathetic portrayal Prager cites Mill's position that imperial rule is only just if it prepares the ruled for independence through enlightened despotism, and that Mill saw this as the only practical way for the imperially governed to become independent.[331]

To critique Prager's view here point by point would be to repeat what I have already said throughout this thesis. As with Tunick discussed above, the particular points above do not complicate the portrayal of Mill in critical literature or the work I have presented in this thesis. Rather, these points fit with a thinker trying to guide the backwards through multiple stages of democratization, development, and modernization. That said I turn to Prager's comparison of Mill's views on intervention and empire to the views of these in the contemporary era which Prager argues are bolder and more prone to advocating imperial intervention without any of Mill's prudence and acuity.[332]

Prager sees imperial intervention in the contemporary world as beyond anything Mill would have condoned or imagined. Prager has in mind contemporary IR scholarship advocating grand cosmopolitanism, political practice such as recent interventions in Kosovo and Iraq, as well as in policy documents such as the *National Security Strategy of the United States* (particularly the doctrine of pre-emptive self-defense) and the *Responsibility to Protect Doctrine* (particularly the weakening of the protection of state sovereignty as obstacle to humanitarian intervention in failed states). I will not get into the details of these here but instead I merely note that Prager, correctly in my view, thinks these examples embody extensive and explicit examples of an imperial willingness to use force by Western states under the justification that it is aimed at improving and protecting the peoples in non-Western states. Of course, contrary to Prager's view, I hold that Mill also embodies this willingness, and in fact was innovator and practitioner of it in modern history.

Nevertheless, Prager endorses a turn to Mill's ideas on intervention and empire in response to concerns over the cosmopolitan denial of the moral standing of non-Western states.[333] Prager does so because in contrast to the contemporary willingness to use imperial intervention as a mode of politics, as outlined above, Prager sees Mill as a prudent and realistic thinker,[334] a realistic thinker, furthermore, who doesn't buy into a grand international law, who sets limits on the use of force, and who only advocates imperial intervention when it is practical and in the interest of the imperialized.[335] Furthermore, Prager thinks that Mill's views are sensibly based on morality and circumstance as opposed to self-interest and abstract law. Hence Prager takes Mill to be prudent with an acuity of vision that should be turned to today.[336] The problem with this turn to Mill, however, is that Prager's portrayal, like all three sympathetic standpoints, misses the significance of Mill's civilizational language, Mill's imperial democratization theorem, and therefore Mill's willingness to use force to pursue civilizational progress.

Prager's is the last of the three sympathetic standpoints taken up in this chapter and it has brought me to an intersection between Mill's imperialism and contemporary imperialism which is beyond the scope of this thesis. Having explicated the sympathetic standpoints and outlined critiques of this literature on Mill and imperialism I hope to have illustrated two things. One is the way in which this literature does not understand Mill's civilizational language. The other is that this literature could benefit from an account of Mill's imperial democratization theorem. Because this sympathetic literature is missing these two components of Mill's relationship to imperialism they provide erroneous critiques of critical literature and misrepresent Mill's relationship to imperialism. These errors lead to a larger misstep in Tunick's and Prager's desire to apply Mill's imperialism to the contemporary world.

Conclusion: Reflections on Further Scholarship

In conclusion it is worth noting that I share Prager's general concern with the contemporary politics of imperial intervention in global politics, particularly with regards to the specific examples she provides. I, however, think Mill is the wrong thinker to turn to in search of options. Aside from the problems of Prager's thin examination of Mill's imperialism, the comparison of Mill's imperialism to contemporary imperial visions to find a course of action away from the latter is ill-advised. One reason is that these contemporary arguments for imperial intervention have a liberal-imperial pedigree that involves Mill's influence.[337]

For example, all of the imperial interventions that Prager refers to are similar to Mill's imperialism in that they claim to be protecting the interest of humanity and to only prescribe force in limited cases when circumstances require it.[338] Moreover, the contemporary focus on illiberal and failed states in which liberal states and non-governmental organizations that are ready, willing, and able can help, develop, modernize, and democratize those who are deemed by them to have improper ways of life and governance is also like Mill's imperialism.[339] Mill's imperialism and contemporary imperialism are also similar in their homologous combination of imperialism, democracy, and principles of good governance that rely on a division of humanity into the properly ordered and the improperly ordered.[340]

Furthermore, that many of the contemporary imperial interveners claim to be motivated by a principle to prevent harm to humanity is also Mill-like in quite specific ways. Both, for example, claim to promote and protect principles of good governance and conceptions of liberty with limits on the use of force. The limits for both Mill's imperialism and contemporary imperialism are that force is only used when it is necessary and moral as opposed to all circumstances when it would be judged as a politically sufficient or advantageous course of action for achieving particular ends.[341]

The vagueness of the limits and the role the imperializer plays as the judge of necessity and morality brings into question the effectiveness and sincerity of these supposed limits. Moreover, that both Millian imperialism and contemporary imperialism limit the use of force while displaying a bold willingness to employ force against those who are deemed to live in improper normative orders (non-civilized cultural, economic, legal, social, and political orders) exemplifies how the language of limits is like a double edged sword in that it is also a language of permissibility for violent aggressive action. Mill's imperialism and contemporary imperialism, the kind Prager is concerned with, are similar and likely related. At the very least they fit together comfortably as one discourse.

That said, in this thesis I have limited myself to clearly outlining the many features of Mill's imperialism and I did so by bringing together the critical standpoint literature with an extensive treatment of Mill's imperial democratization and good governance theorem and with an examination of the sympathetic literature. Through this approach I have identified and crystallized various conceptual relationships that operate in Mill's imperialism. Moreover, this approach has illuminated gaps in the critical literature and shortcomings in the sympathetic literature.

Regarding the former, for example, Melanie White and Jennifer Pitts discuss Mill's ethology as a science of character formation and connect it with his notion of good governance but do not adequately explain the way in which Mill's notion of good governance is an assessment and diagnosis of the form of government needed to best reshape the character of others.[342] In this sense Mill's ethology and notion of good governance are tightly related and can be framed as the same concept. Pitts and White also do not situate the ethological good governance notion within its role as one of three elements that constitute the architecture of Mill's theorem outlined in *Considerations*—imperialism and democracy being the other two essential elements.

Another example of a gap is Parekh's rendering of Mill's division of humanity as a binary.[343] Because once Mill's theorem is identified it is clear that in addition to dividing humanity through his civilizational language in a binary fashion Mill also separates humanity by degrees along a continuum through the civilizational language. The two forms of division provide Mill's theorem with a governmental flexibility to prescribe forms of polities and courses of action based on the fact that a nation is civilized or non-civilized (the binary justification), or based on the fact that this same nation is some degree of hybrid between civilized and non-civilized. Mill's theorem accesses both forms which enables a kind of flexibility in imperial governance of dependencies.

Regarding the sympathetic literature, this approach also illuminated a number of the fundamental problems in the interpretations and accounts provided by these authors. In outlining the theorem, extensively armed with the insights of the critical literature, I have shown the way in which sympathetic literature misreads Mill's civilizational language and is unable to accurately account for Mill's imperialism because these authors are unaware of the connection between the three elements of the architecture of Mill's theorem, which are imperialism, democracy, and good governance. They are also unable to recognize that these three elements go together in modern constitutionalism more broadly. Mark Tunick, for example, sees the enforcement of liberal tolerance as non-imperial because the standards of reason and the standards of civilization instituted through the imposition of rule of law and democracy is applied across humanity equally—equal in the sense that everyone regardless of nationality and culture is treated the same. Since Tunick presumes that Mill and modern constitutionalism protects others in a non-violent way without harming them, even accommodating local practices when they are considered reasonable by foreign governors, he presumes it is not an extensive form of intolerant imperialism.[344] Tunick's position is untenable, however, when *Considerations* is properly assessed as a treatise of Mill's theorem to guide British governors in the reshaping of others through despotic force to pursue a particular vision of civilizational progress developed by Mill from his nineteenth century Victorian English context. Tunick's position and the content of *Considerations* I outlined in my second chapter are clearly not commensurable.

Another example of the way in which recognition of Mill's theorem illuminates shortcomings in sympathetic literature is Carol Prager's view that Mill is a cautious, conservative, and sensible about the use of imperial force compared to contemporary imperial interveners.[345] My examination of Mill's theorem illuminates how inaccurate this portrayal of Mill is given the reality of Mill's theorem and Mill's goal of civilizational progress.

In sum, the second chapter of this thesis is a crucial contribution to the literature on Mill and imperialism. It shows how Mill brings the languages of imperialism, democracy, and good governance together to formulate his theorem outlined in the first four chapters of *Considerations*.[346] It outlines in depth how Mill brings these languages together to promote the gradual training of immature non-European and illiberal nations through despotic force to "walk alone" by means of imposing a series of constitutional orders to reshape the "non-civilized."[347] A major feature of this outline was the identification of Mill's will and ability clause which holds that a nation must have the will and ability to conduct itself in ways that are conducive to particular constitutional orders. For example the civilized, and only the civilized, conduct themselves in ways that are conducive to representative government by satisfying the three conditions of the will and ability clause. I also outlined in some depth that a major precondition for this gradual training and for representative government is, for Mill, the modular commercial development he sees as instituting the necessary material development and collective discipline required for proper moral development. This paragraph here, then, is a synopsis of Mill's blueprint for pursuing civilizational progress for humanity which is more thoroughly outlined in chapter two.

Mill's blueprint is indicative of, and reflects, a broader pattern in Western imperial practice.[348] The broader patterns are the imposing of liberal-democratic constitutionalism including the imposing of modular forms of the rule of law, property rights, economic liberalization including the enforcement of particular trade policies (especially free trade policies), industrial development, and a system of representative government. The latter imposition enforces a separation between the sovereign (the crown) acting through an executive branch of government which manages a partially enfranchised population who vote for representatives that sit in a legislative branch of government.[349] I have outlined in detail how these languages are mutually inclusive in Mill's thought.

In this thesis, however, I have merely examined the recent scholarly engagement with Mill and imperialism and accounted for one specific aspect of Mill's imperialism that to date has escaped focus. Based on what has been outlined in this work I hold, in contrast to predominant and sympathetic literatures, that nobody would do well to follow Mill in his ideas for the improvement of humankind. The emergence of sympathetic standpoints, perhaps Carol Prager's especially, illustrates a need for further critical scholarship on Mill's liberal imperialism and the liberal imperialism that operates in the contemporary world.

Building on the work I carry out in this thesis there is much more to be done. Most pertinently a more thorough history of the influence and continuities of Millian imperialism into the contemporary world should be undertaken. Also histories of resistances to Mill's imperialism and the continuities of these resistance histories from Mill's day through to contemporary resistances would be major contributions to Mill scholarship. Finally, a more thorough critique of the Millian and neo-Millian imperial political visions in their original and contemporary forms is also needed. Ultimately Mill is an imperialist with a theorem for the application of imperialism outlined in *Considerations,* which was informed by his experience as a practitioner and public intellectual of imperial governance.

It is in the hands of present interlocutors to judge and locate the value and the proper place of Mill's imperialism in the contemporary world. My standpoint is that Mill's imperialism, as explicated in this thesis should be rejected as an acceptable module of imposed systematic governance. In my view this form of governance is all too often universalized and imperially imposed as the ideal form of "democracy", "constitutionalism", and "proper government" for all of humanity.

End Notes

[1] *Stanford Encyclopedia of Philosophy*, " John Stuart Mill.". First published in January 2002 with substantive revision on July, 2006. http://plato.stanford.edu/entries/mill/ (April 5, 2007). Other examples of what I would categorize as predominant standpoints include the following works. Nicholas Capaldi, *John Stuart Mill: A Biography* (Cambridge: Cambridge University Press, 2004).; Bruce Kinzer, Ann P. Robson, and John M. Robson. *A Moralist In and Out of Parliament* (Toronto: University of Toronto Press, 1992); Robson, John M. "Civilization and culture as moral concepts," In *The Cambridge Companion to Mill*. Ed. John Skorupski. (Cambridge: Cambridge University Press, 1998), 338-371; John M Robson, *The Improvement of Mankind: The Social and Political Thought of John Stuart Mill*: (Toronto: University of Toronto Press, 1968). Nadia Urbinati. *Mill on democracy: from the Athenian polis to representative government*. (Chicago: University of Chicago Press), 2002. Some of these predominant standpoint scholars seem to be developing what I call sympathetic standpoints. These are standpoints that deny Mill is imperialist, or embrace Mill's liberal imperialism as a just and desirable political theory. For an example of this trend see the recent work by Alan Ryan, "Bureaucracy, Democracy, Liberty: Some Unanswered Questions in Mill's Politics," in *J.S.. Mill's Political Thought: A Bicentennial Reassessment*. Eds. Urbinati, Nadia and Alex Zakaras Cambridge: Cambridge University Press, 2007, 147-165; and also see Nadia Urbinati, "The Many Heads of the Hydra," in *J.S. Mill's Political Thought: A Bicentennial Reassessment*. Eds. Urbinati, Nadia and Alex Zakaras Cambridge: Cambridge University Press, 2007, 66-97. Urbinati

[2] This period is from 1994-2007 and is constituted by the following works. Don Habibi, "The Moral Dimensions of J.S. Mill's Colonialism,." *Journal of Social Philosophy* (Spring 1999); Beate Jahn, "Barbarian Thoughts: imperialism in the philosophy of John Stuart Mill," *Review of International Studies* 31(2005), 599-618; Margaret Khon and Daniel O'Neill, "A Tale of Two Indias: Burke and Mill on Empire and Slavery in the West Indies and America." *Political Theory* 34 (April 2006), 192-228, Uday Mehta, *Liberalism and Empire: A Study in Nineteenth-Century British Liberal Thought* (London: University of Chicago Press, 1999); Peers Moirs and Lynn Zastoupil. Eds. *J.S. Mill's Encounter with India*. (Toronto: University of Toronto Press, 1999); Jennifer Pitts, "James and John Stuart Mill: The Development of Imperial Liberalism in Britain." In *A Turn to Empire: The Rise of Imperial Liberalism in Britain and France*. (Oxford: Princeton University Press, 2005), 123-133; Eddy Souffrant, *Formal Transgressions: John Stuart Mill's Philosophy of International Affairs* (Lanham: Roman and Littlefield 2000); Carol Prager, "Intervention and Empire: John Stuart Mill and International Relations," *Political Studies* (October 2005), 621-640; Mark Tunick,, "Tolerant imperialism: John Stuart Mill's Defense of British Rule in India," *The Review of Politics*,68 (2006), 586-611; Melanie White, "The liberal character of ethological governance." *Economy and Society* 34 (August 2005), 474-494; and Lynn Zastoupil. *John Stuart Mill and India*.(California: Stanford University Press, 1994). In addition to this core literature during this period there are also a number of works that note Mill's relationship to imperialism. These are the following works. See Dipesh Chakrabarty, *Provincializing Europe* (Princeton: Princeton University Press, 2000), 8,9, and 169; Duncan Ivison, *Postcolonial Liberalism* (Cambridge: Cambridge University Press, 2002), 34, 45, and 62; Martti Koskenniemi, *The Gentle Civilizer of Nations: The Rise of International Law: 1870-1960* (Cambridge University Press, 2002) , 23 and 73; and James Tully, "The Imperialism of Modern Constitutionalism," in *The Paradox of Constitutionalism: Constituent Power and Constitutional Form* (Oxford: Oxford University Press, 2007), 327. One precursor to these works is Eileen Sullivan's article "Liberalism and Imperialism: J.S Mill's Defence of the British Empire," *Journal of the History of Ideas* 44:4 (1983): 599-617. For additional works on Mill and imperialism also see Mehta, Pratap, "Liberalism, Nation, and Empire: The Case of J.S. Mill." Paper Presented at the American Political Science Association, San Francisco, 1996; see Georgios Varouxakis, "Empire, Race, Euro-centrism: John Stuart Mill and His Critics," In *Utilitarianism and Empire*; Edited by Bart Shultz and Georgios Varouxakis. Lanham, MD: Lexington Books, 2005; see Karuna Mantena. "Mill and the Imperial Predicament." In *J.S. Mill's Political Thought: A Bicentennial Reassessment*. Eds. Urbinati, Nadia and Alex Zakaras Cambridge: Cambridge University Press, 2007, 298-318; and also see Stephen Holmes, "Making Sense of Liberal Imperialism," in *J.S. Mill's Political Thought: A Bicentennial Reassessment*. Eds. Urbinati, Nadia and Alex Zakaras Cambridge: Cambridge University Press, 2007.

---

[3] See the following works for examples of notions of imperialism being used in Mill scholarship. Jahn, "Barbarian Thoughts," 613 and 617; Souffrant, *Formal Transgression*, 35-36; Tunick, "Tolerant Imperialism," 589-590; and Prager, "Intervention and Empire," 622-623. For a more thorough account of meanings and uses of the terms imperial, imperialist, imperialism, and empire see Robert Young, *Post-colonialism: An Historical Introduction*, 25-43. For a work that outlines different theories of imperialism including classic imperialism and free trade imperialism see Wolfgang Mommsen, *Theories of Imperialism* (London: Weidenfeld and Nicoloson and Random House), 1981, pp. 1-00. Also see Sidney Morgenbesser, "Imperialism: Some Preliminary Distinctions," *Philosophy of Public Affairs* 3:1 (Autumn 1973): 3-44. For other significant scholarship on modern imperialism see the following. Antony Anghie, "The Evolution of International Law: colonial and postcolonial realities," *Third World Quarterly* 27 (2006): 739-753; Antony Anghie, *Imperialism, Sovereignty and the Making of International Law* (Cambridge: Cambridge University Press, 2004); John Darwin, "Imperialism and the Victorians: The Dynamics of Territorial Expansion," *The English Historical Review* 112:447 (June 1997): 614-642; Michael W. Doyle, *Empires* (London: Cornell University Press, 1986); Michael Hardt and Antonio Negri, *Empire* (Cambridge, MA: Harvard University Press, 2001); Michael Hardt and Antonio Negri, *Multitude: War and Democracy in the Age of Empire*(New York: Penguin, 2004); J.A. Hobson, *Imperialism: A Study* (New York: Cosimo, Inc., 2005); Martti Koskenniemi, *The Gentle Civilizer of Nations: The Rise and Fall of International Law 1870-1960* (Cambridge: Cambridge University Press, 2002); John Gallagher and Ronald Robinson "The Imperialism of Free Trade," *The Economic History Review* 6 (January 1953): 1-15;Edward Said, *Culture and Imperialism* (New York: Alfred and Knopp), 1993; Bernard Semmel, *The rise of free trade imperialism; classical political economy, the empire of free trade and imperialism 1750-1850*. (Cambridge: University Press 1970). James Tully, "The Imperialism of Modern Constitutionalism," In *The Paradox of Constitutionalism: Constituent Power and Consitutional Form*, Eds. Martin Loughlin and Neil Walker. Oxford: Oxford University Press, 2007, 315-338; James Tully, "On Law, Democracy and Imperialism," 21st Annual Public Lecture on Law and Society, Faculty of Law, 2005. University of Edinburgh, Edinburgh,Scotland, March 10-11, 2005. Available on the world wide web at http://web.uvic.ca/polisci/tully/publications/Tully%20Presem%20%20Edinburgh%20draft%20criculation%20paper.pdf (July 15, 2007): 1-48; James Tully. "The Nature of the 'New' Imperialism." Lecture givern at the Victoria Colloquium & Demcon Conference, University of Victoria, September 30, 2005. Available on the world wide web at http://web.uvic.ca/polisci/tully/publications/Nature%20of%20the%20New%20Imperialism%2030%209%202005.pdf (July, 15, 2007): 1-9.

[4] Prager, "Intervention and Interference," 622-623. My use of a distinction between intervention and interference within the concept of imperialism that frames this thesis is a modification of a distinction between these terms that is used in this article by Carol Prager.

[5] Mehta, *Liberalism and Empire*, and Pitts, "James and John Stuart Mill...." See these two works for good accounts of this dimension of Millian imperialism.

[6] Mehta's work *Liberalism and Empire* provides the most extensive examination of this dimension. It is also found in Pitts, "James and John Stuart Mill: The Development of Imperial Liberalism in Britain"; and Souffrant, *Formal Transgression*....

[7] This dimension of Millian imperialism is most extensively examined in Souffrant's work *Formal Transgression*. See Souffrant, *Formal Transgression*..., 53-59.

[8] In addition to this thesis, the best accounts of this fundamental dimension of Millian imperialism are in the following works. Jahn, "Barbarian Thoughts"; Mehta, *Liberalism and Empire*; and Pitts, "James and John Stuart Mill: The Development of Imperial Liberalism in Britain." All of the literature on Mill and imperialism provides some account, or at the very least some reference, to Mill's civilizational language. See the works cited in footnote number two of this thesis.

[9] In addition to this thesis the best account of this dimension of Millian imperialism is in Jahn's work "Barbarian Thoughts". It is also noted in Pitts work "James and John Stuart Mill: The Development of Imperial Liberalism in Britain."

[10] Jahn, "Barbarian Thoughts...," Mehta, *Liberalism and Empire*; Tunick, "Tolerant Imperialism,".

[11] The best sources on this dimension of Mill's imperialism are the following. Souffrant, *Formal Transgression*, and White, "The liberal character of ethological governance."

[12] This is noted in different ways in the works by Jahn, "Barbarian Thoughts," Mehta, *Liberalism and Empire*, and Parekh, "Superior Peoples...," Souffrant, *Formal Transgression*, and White "The liberal character of ethological governance."

[13] These three works by Bhikhu Parekh are "Superior Peoples: The Narrowness of liberalism from Mill to Rawls," Times Literary Supplement (February 1994): 11-13; "Liberalism and colonialism: a critique of Locke and Mill." *The Decolonization of Imagination: Culture, Knowledge and Power*. Eds. Jan Nederveen and Bhikhu Parekh. (London: Zen books Ltd., 1995), 81-98; "Decolonizing Liberalism". *The End of "Isms"? . ed*. Alexandras Shtromas. (Oxford: Blackwell, 1994), 105-126. The latter two works are reproductions of "Superior Peoples" in terms of content on Mill.

[14] Parekh, "Superior Peoples...," 11-13.

[15] Parekh, 11.

[16] Parekh, 12-13. Here Parekh refers to liberals such as Joseph Raz, Brian Barry, Ronald Dworkin, and John Rawls as contemporary examples of liberals who have not yet transcended this Millian legacy.

[17] Parekh, 11.

[18] Parekh, 11.

[19] Parekh, 11-13.

[20] Parekh, 11.

[21] Parekh, 11.

[22] Beate Jahn, "Barbarian Thoughts...," 601-604.

[23] Parekh, "Superior Peoples...," 11-12.

[24] Parekh, 11-13.

[25] Parekh 11.

[26] Souffrant, Eddy. *Formal Transgression...*, My treatment of Souffrant's work explains the role of maturity in Millian imperialism in more detail.

[27] Pitts, 133, 135, and 145; and White, "The liberal character of ethological governance," 474-494.

[28] Parekh, 11.

[29] Parekh, 11.

[30] Parekh, 11.

[31] Parekh, 12.

[32] Parekh, 11.

[33] Parekh, 11.

[34] Parekh, 12.

[35] Parekh 12-13.

[36] See Don Habibi, "The Moral Dimensions of...," and Mark Tunick, "Intolerant Imperialism...." The latter is an example of a work that points to Mill's diversity as evidence to his "tolerant imperialism." The former argues that Mill is more tolerant to "white-settler colonies" than with nations of a different "race."

[37] Mehta, Uday Singh. *Liberalism and Empire....*, 26, 31-37, 64, 70-73, 97-106

[38] Mehta, 31 and 81.

[39] Mehta, 26, 31-37, 64, 70-73 and 97-106

[40] Mehta, 70-71.

[41] Mehta, 36-37, and 70-73.

[42] Mehta, 73 and 97-98.

[43] Mehta, 31-32.

[44] Mehta, 32.

[45] Mehta, Mehta, 26, 31-37, 64, 70-73, and 97-106.

[46] Eddy Souffrant. *Formal Transgression...*, 135.

[47] Souffrant, 53-59.

[48] Souffrant, 53-59.

[49] Souffrant, 53-54.

[50] Souffrant, 54.

[51] Souffrant, 55.

[52] John Stuart Mill, "A Few Words on Non-Intervention" [First published in 1859], in volume XXI of *The Collected Works of John Stuart Mill* (33 Volumes), general Ed. John M. Robson. Toronto: University of Toronto press, 1963-1991, 109-124.

[53] Souffrants, *Formal Transgression...*, 59.

[54] Souffrant, 53-54. Souffrant outlines the significant role of this particular conception of maturity in Mill in restricting individuality but finds that it is a vague concept. Souffrant emphasizes that in *On Liberty* Mill does not provide an explicit, complete, and detailed explication of what is constituted in his notion of mature which is problematic for Souffrant since it seems to do so much in his moral philosophy which, in turn, is inextricably linked to Mill's imperialism. Nevertheless Souffrant identifies that Mill does cryptically employ a modular notion of maturity and illustrates its role in Mill's thought when he argues that "Mill's protection of the mature individual's uniqueness is in the end the protection of a conforming person" which is void if an individual's individuality "is thought to deviate from the modular conception of maturity which distinguishes free individuals from others."

[55] Souffrant, 53-59.

[56] Souffrant, 53-59.

[57] Souffrant, 60. The emphasis is added by me.

[58] Michael Igantieff, *Empire Lite: Nation-Building in Bosnia, Kosovo, and Afghanistan*. (Toronto: Penguin, 2003), 2, 90-93 and 96. Neo-Millians certainly take the international community to encompass the successful mature nations of the world and advocate an empire of liberal-democracies. Michael Ignatieff, who I consider to be one example of a neo-Millian, writes that the notion of 'international community' is a fiction that obscures that fact that imperial democratization and nation-building are a result of the decisiveness and militarily power of the United State's which leads a "new imperium of UN administrators who promote liberal-democracy as the ideal polity for humanity. Ignatieff also writes here that imperialism "used to be the white man's burden..." and this "gave it a bad reputation. But imperialism doesn't stop being necessary just because it becomes politically incorrect. Nations sometimes fail, and when they do only outside help—imperial power—can get them back on their feet." Ignatieff adds that imperial is the right word to use even if these border zones are not going to be occupied in perpetuity and ruled as colonies."

[59] See, for example, John Stuart Mill, "A Few Words...."

[60] Pitts, "James and John Stuart Mill...," 123-162.

[61] Pitts, "James and John Stuart Mill...," 123-162.

[62] Jennifer Pitts. *A Turn to Empire...*, 1-254. In addition to her chapter on James and John Stuart Mill which I am discussing here, Pitts also has chapters on Jeremy Bentham, Edmund Burke, and Adam Smith.

[63] Pitts, "James and John Stuart Mill...," 130.

[64] Pitts, 123-162.

[65] Pitts, 123.

[66] Pitts, 124-125.

[67] Pitts, 125-126.

[68] Pitts, 127.

[69] Pitts, 126.

[70] Pitts, 127.

[71] Pitts, 127.

[72] Pitts, 127.

[73] Pitts, 126.

[74] Pitts, 126.

[75] Pitts, 133.

[76] Pitts, 139. Here Pitts responds to the position that Mill's civilizational language is merely what we would expect from anyone in Mill's historical context. She writes thus in reference to the prominent Mill scholar John Robson who I cite as an example of someone with a predominant standpoint on Mill's relationship to imperialism: "Mill's commentators have often regarded his dismissive views of 'uncivilized' peoples has only to be expected of a period, in John Robson's words, 'when ethnography was an amateur pursuit.' What is noticeable about Mill's version of this sort of civilized-savage dichotomy, however, was not that it was based on inadequate ethnography of the day, but that he seems not to have paid much attention to the ethnography that was available." This point by Pitts coupled with her account of Mill's uniquely developed and extensively utilized civilizational language are sufficient to indicate why Robson's view is grossly inadequate.

[77] Pitts, 139 and 144. Pitts takes this point from Pratap Mehta. Pitts also notes how the individual parallels the nation in Mill's thought.

[78] See my sections on Eddy Souffrant's work *Formal Transgression* and Melanie White's work "Liberal ethological governance."

[79] Pitts, 140.

[80] Pitts, 136.

[81] Pitts, 137.

[82] See Jahn, "Barbarian thoughts…;" John Stuart Mill, "Civilization" [First published in 1836]. In *Essays on Politics and Society: The Collected Works of John Stuart Mill Volume XVIII. Ed. John M. Robson. (Toronto: University of Toronto press, 1977), 119-152;* and *John Stuart Mill, Considerations on Representative Government* [First Published in 1861]. In *Essays on Politics and Society: The Collected Works Volume IXX of John Stuart Mill.* Ed. John M. Robson. (Toronto: University of Toronto Press, 1977), 371-576.

[83] Pitts, "James and Stuart Mill…," 137.

[84] Jahn, "Barbarian thoughts…," 599.

[85] Jahn, 599-601.

[86] Jahn, 601-604.

[87] Jahn, 604-607.

[88] Jahn, 607-610.

[89] Jahn, 600.

[90] Jahn, 604.

[91] James Tully, "The Imperialism of Modern Constitutionalism" in *The Paradox of Constitutionalism: Constituent Power and Constitutional Form*, 315-338. This work supports my claim that it would be more apt to frame Mill as articulating an imperial democratization and good governance theory rather than an international relations theory. Tully provides a concise account of the historical imposition of modern constitutionalism through imperialism including the imposition of democratization and good governance as practices of European imperial policy during the modern period in which Mill lived. .

[92] Jahn, "Barbarian thoughts…,"600-601.

[93] Jahn, 602.

[94] Jahn, 615-116.

[95] Jahn, 616.

[96] Jahn, 602.

[97] See the following citations for examples of contemporary democratization works. Carothers, Thomas. *Critical Mission: Essays on Democracy Promotion* (Washington, D.C.: Carnegie Endowment for International Peace), 2004; Larry Diamond and Marc Plattner; eds. *The Global Resurgence of Democracy* Second ed. (Baltimore: John Hopkins), 1996; Larry Diamond. "Promoting Democracy in the 1990s: Actors and Instruments, Issues and Imperatives." *A Report to the Carnegie Commission on Preventing Deadly Conflict* (New York: Carnegie Corporation of New York), 2003;Renske Doorenspleet, *Democratic Transitions: Exploring the Structural Sources of the Fourth Wave* (Boulder: Lynne Rienner Publishers, Inc.), 2005; Samuel Huntington, *The Third Wave: Democratization: Democratization in the Late Twentieth Century* (Oklahoma: University of Oklahoma Press), 1991;Fareed Zakaria, *The Future of Freedom: Illiberal Democracy at Home and Abroad* (New York: W.W. Norton and Company), 2003; Charles Tilly, *Democracy* (Cambridge: Cambridge University Press), 2007.

[98] Jahn, 602-603.

[99] Jahn, 603.

[100] Jahn, 603.

[101] Jahn, 603-610.

[102] White, "Liberal ethological governance…," 483. White notes that "Mill's ambition to develop a science of character formation was never fully realized" and that *Logic* "generated a mild degree of enthusiasm upon its initial publication" it has "continuted to receive minimal attention from subsequent English-speaking generations".

[103] White, Melanie, "The liberal character of ethological governance." *Economy and Society*. 34 (August 2005): 474-494.

[104] White, 475 and 483.

[105] White, 476-477. Here, White also provides a history of the etymology of "ethological governance".

[106] White, 476.

[107] White, 477.

[108] White, 477.

[109] White, 477.

[110] White, 478.

[111] White, 478.

[112] White, 479.

[113] White, 476-479.

[114] White, 475-479.

[115] White, 476. White even connects Mill's ethological governance to Mill's work on *The Subjection of Women* making White the first author to connect Mill's relationship to imperialism with this text otherwise largely embraced and contested over its merits as a work of feminism. It is tied to Mill's civilizational language when White writes thus: "In principle, ethology's potential for reform extends not only to women but also to the lower classes, perceived 'degenerates', colonial subjects and aboriginals who exhibit an inferior character through want of appropriate training and education". White adds that "the difference between English women and colonial subjects is that women's natural character is obscured by the artifice of Victorian society, whereas the character of colonized peoples can claim no such conceit for it ostensibly develops under 'natural' circumstances". The key point here is that in "claiming that English women have an immediate potential for ethological governance that does not extend to colonized peoples, Mill inadvertently reveals a civilizational bias that belies an apparently neutral, and hence scientific, approach to the study of character". See White, 485-486.

[116] White, "Liberal ethological governance...", 483.

[117] Jahn, "Barbarian thoughts..., 602-603; and Mill "*Considerations...*, 371-373, 390-391 and 395-398.

[118] John Stuart Mill,*On Liberty* [First Published in 1859], in volume IXX of *The Collected Works of John Stuart Mill* (33 Volumes), general Ed. John M. Robson, Toronto: University of Toronto press, 1963-1991, 213-292. Also see White, "Liberal ethological governance...,", 474-494.

[119] White, "Liberal ethological governance...," 479-480.

[120] Said, *Culture and Imperialism* (New York: Alfred and Knopp, 1993), 223.

[121] White, "Liberal ethological governance...,"483.

[122] White 477, 475-480, and 489. White explains that it "may be said that a concern for character and consequently ethological governance, has never really left us. As Foucault has remarked, pronouncements on the 'return' of anything are both dangerous and impudent, for such things have usually persisted albeit beneath the surface of social life."

[123] A rare example of a work that frames Mill's liberal imperialism as essentially a democratization theorem is Stephen Holme's recent work "Making Sense of Liberal Imperialism," in *J.S. Mill's Political Thought: A Bicentennial Reassessment*; Eds. Urbinati, Nadia and Alex Zakaras Cambridge: Cambridge University Press, 2007. Holmes, however, does this in an uncritical way emphasizing in his conclusion, on page 346, that Mill's democratization theorem is still, in a contemporary context, a "pertinent theory of the obstacles to democracy." Contemporary democratization thinkers include academics such as Gabriel Almond and Sidney Verba, Samuel Huntington, Larry Diamond as well as popular proponents of a liberal democratization of failed and illiberal states such as Newsweek editor Fareed Zakaria. See the following works for examples of contemporary democratization works. Carothers, Thomas. Critical Mission: Essays on Democracy Promotion (Washington, D.C.: Carnegie Endowment for International Peace), 2004; Larry Diamond and Marc Plattner; eds. *The Global Resurgence of Democracy*, Second ed.(Baltimore: John Hopkins), 1996; Larry Diamond "Promoting Democracy in the 1990s: Actors and Instruments, Issues and Imperatives." *A Report to the Carnegie Commission on Preventing Deadly Conflict* (New York: Carnegie Corporation of New York), 2003;Renske Doorenspleet, *Democratic Transitions: Exploring the Structural Sources of the Fourth Wave.* (Boulder: Lynne Rienner Publishers, Inc.), 2005; Francis Fukuyama, "Liberal Democracy as Global Phenomenon." Political Science and Politics 24:4 (December 1991): 659-664;Francis Fukuyama, *Nation-Building: Beyond Afghanistan and Iraq* (Baltimore: The Johns Hopkins University Press), 2006;Francis Fukuyama, The end of History and the last man. London: Hamish Hamilton 1992; Samuel Huntington, "Clash of Civilizations?" *Foreign Affairs* 72:3 (1993): 22-49; Samuel Huntington, *The Third Wave: Democratization: Democratization in the Late Twentieth Century* (Oklahoma: University of Oklahoma Press), 1991;Fareed Zakaria, *The Future of Freedom: Illiberal*

Democracy at Home and Abroad (New York: W.W. Norton and Company), 2003;Tilly, Charles. *Democracy* (Cambridge: Cambridge University Press), 2007. One work that preceded this field but is often tuned to is Gabriel Almond's and Sidney Verba's, *The Civic Culture: Political Attitudes and Democracy in Five Nations* (Fourth edition. Princeton: Princeton University), 1963. This work in conjunction with 19th century works by Alexis De Tocqueville and more recent works by Robert Putnam are considered the classics of civic virture and "democratic culture." For works that are critical of the democratization field and the practices that are carried out by its practitioners include the following two examples. Boaventura de Sousa Santos Ed. *Democratizing Democracy: Beyond the Liberal Democratic Canon* (London: Verso, 2005); and Beate Jahn,"The Tragedy of Liberal Diplomacy: Democratization, Intervention, Statebuilding (Part I)," *Journal of Intervention and Statebuilding* (March 2007): 87: 106

[124] John Stuart Mill, *Considerations on Representative Government* [First Published in 1861], in volume XVIII of *The Collected Works of John Stuart Mill* (33 Volumes), general Ed. John M. Robson, Toronto: University of Toronto press, 1963-1991, 371-576.

[125] Mill, "A Few Words...," 109-124.

[126] Mill, 109-124.

[127] Mill, *Considerations...*, 373, and 395-396. Mill writes, for example, thus: It is, then impossible to understand the question of the adaptation of forms of government to states of society, without taking into account not only the next step, but all the steps which society has yet to make; both those which can be foreseen, and the far wider indefinite range which is at present out of sight. It follows, that to judge of the merits of forms of government, an ideal must be constructed of the form of government most eligible in itself, that is, which, if the necessary conditions existed for giving effect to its beneficial tendencies, would, more than all others, favour and promote not some one improvement, but all forms and degrees of it. This having been done, we must consider what are the mental conditions of all sorts, necessary to enable this government to realize its tendencies, and what therefore, are the various defects by which a people is made incapable of reaping its benefits. *It would then be possible to construct a theorem of circumstances in which that form of government may wisely be introduced, and also to judge in cases in which it had better not be introduced, what inferior forms of polity will best carry those communities through the intermediate stages which they must traverse before they can become fit for the best form of government.* Emphasis is added by me.

[128] Mill, 373

[129] Mill, 395-396, and 398.

[130] Mill, 374-577. This synopsis is gleaned from this work.

[131] Mill, 371, 390-391, and 396-397.

[132] Mill, 371-373, 390-391 and 395-398.

[133] Mill, 371-373, 390-391 and 395-398.

[134] Tully, "The Imperialism of Modern Constitutionalism," 315-338. Beyond just Mill, this work by Tully provides an account of how modern imperialism, modern democracy, and modern concepts of good governance feature in the Western imperial practice of modern constitutionalism. Regarding Mill specifically, Alan Ryan has recently denied that Mill is in an imperialist on the basis that he was committed to good government and not national glory and, thus, Mill could not be an imperialist. For this argument see Ryan's work Bureaucracy, Democracy, Liberty: Some Unanswered Questions in Mill's Politics." In *J.S. Mill's Political Thought: A Bicentennial Reassessment*. Eds. Urbinati, Nadia and Alex Zakaras Cambridge: Cambridge University Press, 2007, 150-151. Ryan does not illustrate why despotic imposition by a foreign power under the auspices of good government and benevolent despotic rule are mutually exclusive from imperialism. Ryan suggests colonialism is only imperial when it is motivated by a quest for national glory and the expansion of territory. Making this argument requires an extensively narrow concept of imperialism.My thesis here, and Tully's work above, elucidate how it is that the language of good government is not mutually excusive from notions and practices of imperialism.

[135] Mill, *Considerations...*, 374-421. These are forms of government Mill discusses in these pages which encompasses the first four chapters of *Considerations*. My outline of these seven forms are abstracted form these pages.

[136] Mill, *Considerations*, 398..

[137] Mill, *Considerations*, 386-387, 389, 391-398. Also see my discussion of Melanie White's work on Mill and ethological governance in this thesis.

[138] Mill, *Considerations...*, 376.

[139] Mill, 413.

[140] Mill, 380.

[141] Mill, 376-377.

[142] Mill's portrayal of indigenous communities in North America is a false and seemly purely constructed misrepresentation of the plurality of indigenous orders that existed and continue to exist. For works that more accurately recognize and discuss a plurality of indigenous constitutional orders in North America see the following works. John Borrows."Indigenous Legal Traditions in Canada." *Journal of Law and Policy* 19 (2005): 167-220; John Borrows, *Recovering Canada: The Resurgence of Indigenous Law* (Toronto: University of Toronto Press, 2002); and James Tully, *Strange Multiplicity: Constitutionalism in an age of diversity*. (Cambridge: Cambridge University Press, 1995). It should be noted that there is a liberal-tradition of such false representations of indigenous orders that goes back to Immanuel Kant and John Locke. For two primary works on Locke and Kant that provide similar, but not synonymous, misrepresentations of indigenous peoples in arguments for a "civilizing" approach to Euro-Indigenous relations see the following works. Immanuel Kant, *Political Writings*. 2nd. Edition. Ed. Hans Reiss. (Cambridge: Cambridge University Press, 2005); John Locke, *Second treatise of government*. Ed. By C.B. Macpherson. (Indianapolis: Hackett Pub, 1980). For two secondary works that examine this aspect of Locke see the following. Barbara Arneil, *John Locke and America: the defence of English colonialism* (Oxford, England: Clarendon Press, 1996); and James Tully, *An Approach to Political Philosophy: Locke in Contexts*. Cambridge: (Cambridge University Press, 1993). For commentary on Mill's misrepresentation of indigenous peoples of India see, for example, Dipesh Chakrabarty, *Provincializing Europe*, and Uday Mehta, *Liberalism and Empire*.

[143] Mill, 376-377.

[144] Mill, 374-377, and 382.

[145] Mill, 376-377.

[146] Mill, 376-377.

[147] Mill, 377-378.

[148] Mill, 377.

[149] Mill, 377.

[150] Mill, 377.

[151] See Mill, *Considerations...*, and Mill "A Few Words...."

[152] Mill, *Considerations...*, 376-377.

[153] Mill, 387-388.

[154] Mill, 387-388.

[155] See Habibi, "Moral Dimensions....;" Jahn, "Barabrian thoughts....," and Mill, "Civilization." Also see my discussions of this point in "Chapter One" and in the last section of "Chapter Two" of this thesis.

[156] Mill, *Consideration*, 383-384.

[157] Mill, *Considerations*, 384-388.

[158] Mill, *Considerations*, 384-388.

[159] See Habibi, "Moral Dimensions....;" Jahn, "Barabrian thoughts....," and Mill, "Civilization." Also see my discussions of this point in "Chapter One" and in the last section of "Chapter Two" of this thesis. These two exigencies of good government in Mill's thought actually mirror two developmental exigencies of his concept of civilization which includes moral development and material development. In this case moral development necessarily includes material development in much the same way that progress necessarily includes order, that is too much or too little material development can be an obstacle to moral development and, therefore, to civilizational progress. Furthermore, Mill posits that too much or too little material development can harm moral development. Again Mill is quite concerned with the relationship between moral development and material development—this aspect is discussed further in this chapter when I discuss Mill's essay "Civilization".

[160] See, for example, Mill, *Considerations...*; and Mill "Civilization." Mill's discussion of regression, stationariness, and progress are discussed throughout these works.

[161] Mill, *Considerations*, 386-387, 389 and 391.

[162] Mill, 388.

[163] Mill, 388-392.

[164] Mill, 389.

[165] Mill, 390-391.

[166] Mill, 395-396.

[167] Mill, 398. The emphasis is mine.

[168] Mill, 390-391 and 398.

[169] Mill, *Considerations*, 398.

[170] Mill, 401.

[171] Mill, 401.

[172] Mill, 401.

[173] Mill, 404.

[174] Mill, 404.

[175] Mill, 404.

[176] Mill, 404.

[177] Mill, 404.

[178] See, for example, Mill, *Considerations*, 374-377, and 382. Mill distinguishes rational choice from irrational choice on page 382 in regards to forms of government which means, that the civilized also must choose the right form of government to satisfy the will and ability clause outlined on pages 374-377.

[179] Mill, 406-407. Mill writes that the "This question really depends upon a still more fundamental one— viz. which of two common types of character, for the general good of humanity, it is most desirable should predominate—the active, or the passive type; that which struggles against evils, or that which endures them; that which bends to circumstances, or that which endeavors to make circumstances bend to itself."

[180] Mill, 406-407.

[181] Mill, 407.

[182] Mill, 408. "Mill has a footnote here to qualify his civilizational language regarding the European nations. He writes thus: "I limit the expression to past time, because I would say nothing derogatory of a great, and now at least a free, people, who are entering into the general movement of European progress with a vigour which bids fair to make up rapidly the ground they have lost. No one can doubt what Spanish intellect and energy are capable of; and their faults as a people are chiefly those for which freedom and industrial ardour are a real specific."

[183] Mill, *Considerations*, 409.

[184] Mill, 409-410.

[185] Mill, 410. Here Mill writes thus: "Inactivity, unaspiringness, absence of desire, are a more fatal hindrance to improvement than any misdirection of energy; and are that through which alone, when existing the mass, any very formidable misdirection by an energetic few becomes possible. It is this, mainly, which retains in a savage or semi-savage state the great majority of the human race."

[186] Mill, *Considerations*, 410.

[187] It should be noted that any strong position on the dichotomous question of whether or not Mill's prescription of representative government is particular or universal is futile in its simplicity because Mill's prescription is both particular and universal in Mill's theorem. It is particular to and necessary for civilized peoples but incompatible for non-civilized people. Moreover, all non-civilized people should be civilized and therefore become willing and able to acquire representative government. Representative government is therefore universalized as an ideal-form of government for all of humanity in the modern world but this is an ideal that should eventually be achieved in practice and this requires that non-civilized peoples go through the necessary stages and steps including particular forms of external despotic government applied against their will.

[188] Mill, *Considerations*, 413-421.

[189] Mill, 413.

[190] Mill, 418.

[191] Mill, 418-419.

[192] Mill, 546-552.

[193] Mill, 446.

[194] Mill, 547.

[195] Mill, 549.

[196] Mill, 549-550.

[197] Mill, 550.

[198]Mill, *Considerations,* 549. Here Mill writes thus: "Experience proves, that it is possible for one nationality to merge and be absorbed in another: and when it was originally an inferior and more backward portion of the human race, the absorption is greatly to its advantage. Nobody can suppose that it is not more beneficial to a Breton, or a Basque of French Navarre, to be brought into the current of the ideas and feelings of a highly civilized and cultivated people—to be a member of the French nationality, admitted on equal terms to all the privileges of French citizenship, sharing the advantages of French protection, and the dignity and prestige of French power—than to sulk on his own rocks, the half-savage relic of past times, revolving in his own little mental orbit, without the participation or interest in the general movement of the world. The same remark applies to the Welshman or the Scottish Highlander, as members of the British nation."

[199] Mill, *Considerations,* 551-552.

[200] Mill, 553-561. Although this thesis does not attempt to provide an account of why the British colonized others through imperialism, this passage provides an opportunity for a note on the role of economics in Mill's imperial mission. First of all, this passage illustrates that Mill thinks it is just for the empire to appropriate the land of indigenous peoples and do with it what the Empire needs to in order to promote "civilizational progress" including appropriating indigenous land, reallocating the land exclusively to the settler-community, or keeping the land under imperial dominion for the interest of all imperial subjects. For Mill, material development of colonial populations was a crucial aspect of his "civilizing mission" because he thought it was necessary for moral development as I outlined in chapter one, which also gets thoroughly discussed in my outline of Mill's essay "Civilization." Moreover, Mill consistently promotes his economic principles of free trade, commercial development, and the disciplining of population to create a wage labour-force. Hence, although Mill distinguished his imperialism from plunder imperialism he still, in many ways, was a supporter of economic-free trade imperialism. Mill's advocacy of imposing particular English-inspired constitutionalism, as *the* form of "rule of law, on those he wanted to "train" to "walk alone" entails the key strategy of instituting the type of property rights and land enclosure that provide the British empire and its settler subjects with wealth; but also, importantly for Mill, such property policies provide a push towards "material progress." There is then a point of contact between Mill's economic imperialism and Mill's imperial imposition of modern constitutionalism to discipline and reshape the character of indigenous populations in British dependencies. For an account of the role of property law, land enclosure, and the creation of modernity see John Weaver, *The Great Land Rush and the Making of the Modern World: 1650-1900.* Montreal: McGill-Queen's University Press, 2003. Also see John McLaren, A.R. Buck and Nancy E. Wright, eds. *Despotic Dominion: Property Rights in British Settler Societies* (Vancouver: UBC Press, 2005).

[201] Mill, 559.

[202] Mill, 557-558.

[203] Mill, 562.

[204] Parekh "Superior Peoples...;" and Tunick "Intolerant Imperialism...." Both works discuss Mill's relationship with racism.

[205] Mill, *Considerations,* 562-563.

[206] Mill, 563.

[207] Mill, 563-566.

[208] Mill, 563-564.

[209] Mill, 565.

[210] Mill, 568-570.

[211] This is noted in Prager's "Intervention and Empire...;" Tunick's "Tolerant Imperialism...."

[212] Mill, *Considerations,* 395-398..

[213] Mill, "A Few Words on Non-Intervention", 118.

[214] John Stuart Mill, "A Few Words on Non-Intervention...," 109-124.

[215] Mill, "A Few Words...", 113-118. For a historical work on the history Suez Canal see Karabell Zachary, *Parting the Desert: The Creation of the Suez Canal.* (New York: Alfred & Knopf), 2003.

[216] Mill, 113-118.

[217] Mill, 113-118.

[218] Mill, 113-118.

[219] Mill, 116-117.

[220] Mill, 113-118.
[221] Mill, 113-118.
[222] Mill, 118-124.
[223] Mill, 118-124.
[224] Mill, 118-124.
[225] Mill, 113.
[226] Mill, 113.
[227] Mill, 121-124.
[228] Mill, 109.
[229] Mill, 109.
[230] Mill, 109.
[231] Mill, 109.
[232] Mill, 113.
[233] Mill, 115.
[234] Mill, 116.
[235] Mill, 118-119.
[236] Mill, 118.
[237] Mill, 119.
[238] Mill, 119-127.
[239] Mill, 119-220.
[240] Mill, 121-124.
[241] Mill, 121.
[242] Mill, 121.
[243] Mill, 122.
[244] Mill, 122.
[245] Mill, 122.
[246] Mill, 123-124.
[247] Mill, 123-124.
[248] John Stuart Mill, "Civilization" [First Published in 1836], in volume XVIII of *The Collected Works of John Stuart Mill* (33 Volumes), general Ed. John M. Robson, Toronto: University of Toronto press, 1963-1991, 119.
[249] Mill, 119.
[250] Mill, 119.
[251] Mill, 119.
[252] Mill, 119.
[253] Mill, 119.
[254] Mill, 119-147.
[255] Mill, 135-147.
[256] Mill, 121.
[257] Mill, 129.
[258] Mill, 129.
[259] Mill, 130.
[260] Mill, 129-133.
[261] Mill, 130-132.
[262] Mill, 132.
[263] Mill, 119.
[264] Mill, 135-136.
[265] Mill, 136.
[266] Kohn and O'Neill citation, " A Tale of Two Indias…," 192-228.
[267] "Tunick, "Tolerant Imperialism…," 586-611.
[268] Prager, "Intervention and Empire…, 621-640. Too additional works that provide sympathetic standpoint arguments are recent works by Alan Ryan and Nadia Urbinati. Alan Ryan, in response to critical standpoints, argues that these critics have overreacted to Mill's relationship to empire. Ryan also argues that Mill is not imperialist because Mill did not advocate imposition on the basis of national glory for the ends of territorial expansion but rather advocated benevolent despotism for the ends of good government.

The problem with Ryan's argument is that good governance and imperialism are not mutually exclusive, as my work has illuminated. Another problem with Ryan's standpoint is that his conception of imperialism is incredibly narrow suggesting that only imposition for the naked self-interested ends of national glory and territorial expansion constitute "imperialism." See Alan Ryan, Bureaucracy, Democracy, Liberty: Some Unanswered Questions in Mill's Politics," In *J.S. Mill's Political Thought: A Bicentennial Reassessment*, Eds. Urbinati, Nadia and Alex Zakaras Cambridge: Cambridge University Press, 2007, 147-165.
Nadia Urbinati makes quite similar arguments as Ryan. For example, she also suggests that critical standpoint theorists have overreacted to Mill's imperialism and argues that Mill was not an imperialist because he advocated against rule by the government of foreign peoples and instead argued for the benevolent governance of others by foreign governors. Urbinati suggests that critical standpoint scholars have too quickly rushed to the conclusion that Mill is imperialist because they have missed an important difference between Mill being interested in imperial government and Mill being interested in paternal good governance. Here Urbinati also seems to implicitly subscribe to a narrow concept of imperialism. It seems, for her, imperialism only constitutes direct political rule by the government of a foreign people and, ergo, 'paternal depotism' by "nonpolitical agencies," such as the East India Company, are not the same as imperialism. Urbinati frames Mill has guilty of advocating "colonialism as capitalist exploitation" but not guilty of advocating "*imperialism* as the political domination by the government of a capitalist country." Urbinati's view is not only inconsistent with what I have illustrated in this thesis (that Mill prescribes many forms of imperialism in a variety of ways) but it is also inconsistent with Michael Waltzer's accurate point that "Mill's ambition for his country is very grand...he wants Britain to be not only a beacon of freedom but an active political and, if necessary, military agent" of freedom. See Nadia Urbinati, "The Many Heads of the Hydra," in *J.S. Mill's Political Thought: A Bicentennial Reassessment*. Eds. Urbinati, Nadia and Alex Zakaras Cambridge:Cambridge University Press, 2007, 66-97; also See Michael Walzer's, "Mill's 'A Few Words on Non-Intervention': A Commentary." In *J.S. Mill's Political Thought: A Bicentennial Reassessment*. Eds. Urbinati, Nadia and Alex Zakaras Cambridge: Cambridge University Press, 2007, 356.

[269] Kohn and O'Neill, "A Tale of Two Indias...," 192-228.
[270] Kohn and O'Neill, 192-193.
[271] Kohn and O'Neill, 192-193.
[272] Kohn and O'Neill, 192-193.
[273] Kohn and O'Neill, 192-193.
[274] Kohn and O'Neill, 193.
[275] Kohn and O'Neill, 206.
[276] Kohn and O'Neill, 206.
[277] Kohn and O'Neill, 213-217.
[278] Kohn and O'Neill, 217.
[279] Kohn and O'Neill, 206.
[280] Kohn and O'Neill, 206.
[281] Kohn and O'Neill, 209.
[282] Kohn and O'Neill, 217.
[283] Kohn and O'Neill, 209.
[284] Kohn and O'Neill, 210-211.
[285] Kohn and O'Neill, 210-211.
[286] Kohn and O'Neill, 210-211.
[287] Mill, "Civilization", 119-152.
[288] Kohn and O'Neill, 217-218
[289] Kohn and O'Neill, 217-218.
[290] Mark Tunick, "Tolerant Imperialism...," 586-611.
[291] Tunick, 588-589, and 611.
[292] Tunick, 588-589, and 611.
[293] Tunick, 611.
[294] Tunick, 589-600.
[295] Tunick, 589-600.
[296] Tunick, 589-591.
[297] Tunick, 591-611.
[298] Tunick, 589-611.

[299] Tunick, 586.
[300] Tunick, 589-600..
[301] Tunick, 587-589.
[302] Tunick, 587-589.
[303] Tunick, 591-594.
[304] Tunick, 588-589.
[305] Tunick, 588-589.
[306] Tunick, 588-589.
[307] Tunick, 589.
[308] Tunick, 601-602.
[309] Tunick, 601.
[310] Tunick, 602.
[311] Tunick, 602-603.
[312] Parekh, "Superior....," 11-13
[313] Mehta, *Liberalism and Empire*....
[314] Tunick, 586-611.
[315] Tunick, 586-611
[316] Tunick, 586.
[317] Mill, *Considerations*...,395-398.
[318] Prager, "Intervention and Empire...," 621-622. Prager accounts for this lack of attention on Mill by the English school writing thus: "Yet, by and large, Mill's views on intervention and interference, pivotal to so many vital issues in international relations, have not received the attention they warrant, a surprising fact given his extraordinary stature. One reason might be Mill's focus. On the one hand, the English school has been most vigorously engaged with the notion of international order, albeit often predicated on the principle of non-interference. Other members of the English School have recently advanced a cosmopolitan vision committed to universal human rights, and government and ecological standards. On the other hand, whilst Mill was primarily concerned with intervention, he considered the shape of international order obliquely, if at all. Another possible reason for his neglect is his association with the East India Company, which provided his livelihood for virtually all his working life, evidence to some that he was a fervent supporter of empire, until recently an unthinkable position. Notwithstanding, it is a tribute to Mill's acuity that he was drawn to intractable international dilemmas and that he identified tensions that will always need to be respected. To the extent that Mill's perspective is present in today's discourse, it is largely in the writing of Michael Walzer." Waltzer himself views Mill differently, has a thinker that would approve of a military intervention in Iraq and he argues that Mill would be heartened by the growth of a civil society of nongovernmental organizations that are in the business of "regime change." See Waltzer's work "Mill's 'A Few Words on Non-Intervention': A Commentary," In *J.S. Mill's Political Thought: A Bicentennial Reassessment*, Eds. Urbinati, Nadia and Alex Zakaras Cambridge: Cambridge University Press, 2007, 347-356.
[319] Prager, 621.
[320] Prager, 622.
[321] Parger, 622.
[322] Prager, 622.
[323] Prager, 623.
[324] Prager, 629.
[325] Prager, 623.
[326] Prager, 628.
[327] Prager, 626-629.
[328] Prager, 631.
[329] Prager, 631.
[330] Prager, 631.
[331] Prager, 631.
[332] Prager, 634-638.
[333] Prager, 633-638.
[334] Prager, 621-638. In asserting that Mill held a prudent and cautious view of imperialism and would not endorse the type of intervention the U.S. is carrying out in Iraq, which cuts against my interpretation that

Mill was an advocate of extensive intervention and interference, Carol Prager points to Michael Waltzer as a thinker who embodies Mill's sensible ideas in the contemporary world. Yet Waltzer recently emphasized, *contra* Prager, that Mill would endorse intervention in Iraq for democratization purposes but would merely want the operation to have been carried out with more will and ability on behalf of the imperializers. Waltzer adds that Mill would be "heartened" by the growth of a civil society that is interested in using interference to carry out "regime change." Waltzer's interpretation of Mill's "A Few Words on Non-Intervention" seems to fit with my reading more than Prager's. The difference between myself and Michael Waltzer is that I explicitly acknowledge that I am normatively opposed to the imperialism of Millian democratization and interventionism whereas it is not clear in this article whether Waltzer adheres to what he calls the "Millian program." Regarding Prager see "Intervention and Empire...;" regarding Waltzer see his work, "Mill's 'A Few Words on Non-Intervention": A Commentary,' In *J.S. Mill's Political Thought: A Bicentennial Reassessment*. Eds. Urbinati, Nadia and Alex Zakaras Cambridge: Cambridge University Press, 2007, 347-356.

[335] Prager, 621-638.

[336] Prager, 621-638.

[337] See Parekh's and Jahn's works for contemporary literature that discusses this historical and theoretical link.

[338] See the following documents. ICISS. *Responsibility to Protect: Report of the International Commission on Intervention and State Sovereignty*. 2001. http://www.iciss.ca/pdf/Commission-Report.pdf (February 28,2007); United States, 2006; *and* United States, *National Security Strategy of the United States*. http://www.whitehouse.gov/nsc/nss/2006/ (October 10, 2006); and the United States, 2002. *National Security Strategy of the United States*. http://www.whitehouse.gov/nsc/nss.html (October 10, 2006).

[339] See the following work for commentary on the *Responsibility to Protect Doctrine*, Oman, Natalie. "A Critical Assessment of the Responsibility to Prevent". Unpublished manuscript, 2007. Also see Michael Byers, *Warlaw: Understanding International Law and Armed Conflict* (Vancouver: Douglas and McIntyre, 2005).

[340] Tully, The Imperialism of Modern Constitutionalism, " In *The Paradox of Constitutionalism: Constituent Power and Constitutional Form*, Eds. Martin Loughlin and Neil Walker. Oxford: Oxford University Press, 2007, 315-338.

[341] See Prager, "Intervetnion and Empire...;" Omon, "A Critical Assessment," The U.S., *NSS*, and the ICSS, *Responsibility to Protect*. Also see Michael Byers, *War Law: Understanding International Law and Armed Conflict* (Vancouver: Douglas and McIntyre), 2005. This has a discussion of the imperial utility of the doctrine.

[342] See White "Liberal ethological...;" and Pitts, "James and John Stuart...."

[343] See Parekh, "Superior Peoples...."

[344] See Tunick, "Intolerant Imperialism...."

[345] See Prager, "Intervention and Empire..."

[346] Mill, *Considerations...*, 395-398.

[347] Mill *Considerations...*, 395-398.

[348] See two works by James Tully. "The Imperialism of Modern Constitutionalism, " In *The Paradox of Constitutionalism: Constituent Power and Constitutional Form*, Eds. Martin Loughlin and Neil Walker. Oxford: Oxford University Press, 2007, 315-338; "On Law, Democracy and Imperialism," 21st Annual Public Lecture on Law and Society, Faculty of Law, 2005. University of Edinburgh, Edinburgh, Scotland, March 10-11, 2005. Available on the world wide web at http://web.uvic.ca/polisci/tully/publications/Tully%20Presem%20-%20Edinburgh%20draft%20criculation%20paper.pdf (July 15, 2007), 1-48.

[349] Tully, "The Imperialism of...," These and other broader patterns are outlined by James Tully in his recent work "The Imperialism of Modern Constitutionalism." In this work Tully outlines the way modern constitutionalism and its global impositions are enclosed by the imperialism of Western modernity and correctly points to Mill as an important canonical thinker of the theory and practice of the imperialism of modern constitutionalism. Tully shows how imperialism, democracy, good governance, and notions of progress are mutually inclusive languages in which the imperial imposition of particular forms of governance continues to be predicated.

Bibliography

Almond, Gabriel A. and Sidney Verba. *The Civic Culture: Political Attitudes and Democracy in Five Nations.* Fourth edition. Princeton: Princeton University, 1963.

Anghie, Antony. "The Evolution of International Law: colonial and postcolonial realities." *Third World Quarterly* 27 (2006): 739-753.

----------. *Imperialism, Sovereignty and the Making of International Law* Cambridge: Cambridge University Press, 2004.

Armitage, David. *The Ideological Origins of the British Empire*: Cambridge University Press, 2002.

Arneil, Barbara. *John Locke and America: the defence of English colonialism.* Oxford, England: Clarendon Press, 1996.

Baum, Bruce. "Feminism, Liberalism and Cultural Pluralism: J. S. Mill on Mormon Polygamy" *Journal of Political Philosophy* 5:3 (1997): 230–253.

----------. "Freedom, power and public opinion: J.S. Mill on the public sphere." *History of Political Thought* 22:3 (2001): 501-524.

----------. "J.S. Mill's conception of economic freedom". *History of Political Thought* 20 :3(1999), 494-530.

----------. *Rereading Power and Freedom in J.S. Mill.* Toronto: University of Toronto Press, 2000.

Bearce, George. *British Attitudes Towards: 1784-1858.* Oxford University Press, 1961.

Beitz, Charles R. *Political Theory and International Relations.* Princeton: Princeton University Press, 1979.

Bell, Duncan, ed. *Victorian Visions of Global Order: Empire and International Relations in Nineteenth-Century Political Thought.* Cambridge: Cambridge University Press, 2008.

Bellamy, Richard. *Victorian Liberalism: Nineteenth-century political thought and practice.* London: Routledge, 1990.

Borrows, John. "Indigenous Legal Traditions in Canada." *Journal of Law and Policy* 19 (2005): 167-220.

----------. *Recovering Canada: The Resurgence of Indigenous Law*. Toronto: University of Toronto Press, 2002.

Bowden, Brett. "In the Name of Progress and Peace; The 'Standard of Civilization' and the Universalizing Project." *Alternatives* 29 (2004): 43-46.

Byers, Michael. *War Law: Understanding International Law and Armed Conflict*. Vancouver: Douglas and McIntyre, 2005.

Capaldi, Nicholas. *John Stuart Mill: A Biography*. Cambridge: Cambridge University Press, 2004.

Carothers, Thomas. *Critical Mission: Essays on Democracy Promotion*. Washington, D.C.: Carnegie Endowment for International Peace, 2004.

Chakrabarty, Dipesh. *Provincializing Europe*. Princeton: Princeton University Press, 2000.

Courtney, W.L. *Life of John Stuart Mill*. Toronto: W.J Gage and Co., 1889.

Cowling, Maurice. *Mill and Liberalism*. Cambridge: Cambridge University Press, 1990.

Darwin, John. "Imperialism and the Victorians: The Dynamics of Territorial Expansion." *The English Historical Review* 112:447 (June 1997): 614-642.

Diamond, Larry and Marc Plattner; eds. *The Global Resurgence of Democracy*. Second ed. Baltimore: John Hopkins, 1996.

Diamond, Larry. "Promoting Democracy in the 1990s: Actors and Instruments, Issues and Imperatives." *A Report to the Carnegie Commission on Preventing Deadly Conflict*. New York: Carnegie Corporation of New York, 2003.

Donner, Wendy. *The Liberal Self: John Stuart Mill's Moral and Political Philosophy*. London: Cornel University Press, 1991.

Doorenspleet, Renske. *Democratic Transitions: Exploring the Structural Sources of the Fourth Wave*. Boulder: Lynne Rienner Publishers, Inc., 2005.

Doyle, Michael W. *Empires*. London: Cornell University Press, 1986.

Fukuyama, Francis. "Liberal Democracy as Global Phenomenon." *Political Science and Politics* 24:4 (December 1991): 659-664.

----------. *Nation-Building: Beyond Afghanistan and Iraq*. Baltimore: The Johns Hopkins University Press, 2006.

----------. The *end of History and the last man*. London: Hamish Hamilton, 1992.

Gallagher, John and Ronald Robinson "The Imperialism of Free Trade. " *The Economic History Review* 6 (January 1953): 1-15.

Glassman, Peter. *The Evolution of a Genius*. Gainesville: University of Florida, 1985.

Gong, Gerrit W. *The Standard of 'Civilization' in International Society*. Oxford: Clarendon Press, 1984.

Habibi, Don. "The Moral Dimensions of J.S. Mill's Colonialism." *Journal of Social Philosophy* 30 (Spring 1999): 125-146.

Hallberg, Charles. *The Suez Canal: Its History and Diplomatic Importance* [First published in 1931]. New York: Octagon Books, 1974.

Hardt, Michael and Antonio Negri. *Empire*. Cambridge, MA: Harvard University Press, 2001.

----------. *Multitude: War and Democracy in the Age of Empire*. New York: Penguin, 2004.

Hobson, J.A. *Imperialism: A Study*. New York: Cosimo, Inc., 2005.

Holmes, Stephen. "Making Sense of Liberal Imperialism." In *J.S. Mill's Political Thought: A Bicentennial Reassessment*. Eds. Urbinati, Nadia and Alex Zakaras Cambridge: Cambridge University Press, 2007.

Huntington, Samuel. "Clash of Civilizations?" *Foreign Affairs* 72:3 (1993): 22-49.

----------. *The Third Wave: Democratization in the Late Twentieth Century*. Oklahoma: University of Oklahoma Press, 1991.

ICISS. *Responsibility to Protect: Report of the International Commission on Intervention and State Sovereignty*. 2001. http://www.iciss.ca/pdf/Commission-Report.pdf (February 28,2007).

Ignatieff, Michael. *Empire Lite: Nation-Building in Bosnia, Kosovo, and Afghanistan*. Toronto: Penguin, 2006.

Ivison, Duncan. *Postcolonial Liberalism*. Cambridge: Cambridge University Press, 2002.

Jahn, Beate. "Barbarian Thoughts: imperialism in the philosophy of John Stuart Mill." *Review of International Studies* 31 (2005): 599-618.

----------. "The Tragedy of Liberal Diplomacy: Democratization, Intervention, Statebuilding (Part I)." *Journal of Intervention and Statebuilding* (March 2007): 87-106.

----------. "The Tragedy of Liberal Diplomacy: Democratization, Intervention, Statebuilding (Part II)." Journal of Intervention and Statebuilding (June 2007): 211-229.

Kant, Immanuel. *Political Writings*. 2nd. Edition. Ed. Hans Reiss. Cambridge: Cambridge University Press, 2005.

Kinzer, Bruce, Ann P. Robson, and John M. Robson. *A Moralist In and Out of Parliament*. Toronto: University of Toronto Press, 1992.

Kohn, Margaret and Daniel O'Neill. "A Tale of Two Indias: Burke and Mill on Empire and Slavery in the West Indies and America." *Political Theory* 34 (April 2006): 192-228.

Koskenniemi, Martti. *The Gentle Civilizer of Nations: The Rise and Fall of International Law 1870-1960*. Cambridge: Cambridge University Press, 2002.

Laine, Michael ed. *A Cultivated Mind: Essays on J.S. Mill Presented to John M. Robson*. Toronto: University of Toronto Press, 1991.

Levin, Michael. *J.S. Mill on Civilization and Barbarism*. London: Routledge, 2004.

Locke, John. *Second treatise of government*. Ed. By C.B. Macpherson. Indianapolis: Hackett Pub, 1980.

Lyons, David ed. *Mill's Utilitarianism: Critical Essays*. Lanham, Marlyland: Rowman and Littefield Publishers Inc., 1997.

McLaren, John, A.R. Buck and Nancy E. Wright. Eds. *Despotic Dominion: Property Rights in British Settler Societies*. Vancouver: UBC Press, 2005.

Mill, John Stuart. *The Collected Works of John Stuart Mill* (33 volumes). General ed. John M. Robson. Toronto, University of Toronto Press, 1963-1991.

----------."A Few Words on Non-Intervention" [First published in 1859]. In volume XXI of *The Collected Works of John Stuart Mill* (33 Volumes). General Ed. John M. Robson. Toronto: University of Toronto press, 1963-1991, 109-124.

----------. *Autobiography* [First Published in 1873]. In volume of I of *The Collected Works of John Stuart Mill* (33 Volumes). General Ed. John M. Robson Toronto. University of Toronto press, 1963-1991, 1-290.

----------. "Civilization" [First Published in 1836]. In volume XVIII of *The Collected Works of John Stuart Mill* (33 Volumes). General Ed. John M. Robson. Toronto: University of Toronto press, 1963-1991, 119-152.

----------. *Considerations on Representative Government* [First Published in 1861]. In volume XVIII of *The Collected Works of John Stuart Mill* (33 Volumes). General Ed. John M. Robson. Toronto: University of Toronto press, 1963-1991, 371-576.

----------. *On Liberty* [First Published in 1859]. In volume IXX of *The Collected Works of John Stuart Mill* (33 Volumes). General Ed. John M. Robson. Toronto: University of Toronto press, 1963-1991, 213-292.

----------. "Nature." Essay 1 of the *Three Essays on Religion*. [First Published in 1874]. In volume X of *The Collected Works of John Stuart Mill* (33 Volumes). General Ed. John M. Robson. Toronto: University of Toronto press, 1963-1991, 373-402.

----------. "The Negro Question" [First published in 1850].]. In volume XXI of *The Collected Works of John Stuart Mill* (33 Volumes). General Ed. John M. Robson. Toronto: University of Toronto press, 1963-1991, 87-95.

----------. *Principles of Political* Economy [First Published in 1848]. In volumes II-III of *The Collected Works of John Stuart Mill* (33 Volumes). General Ed. John M. Robson. Toronto: University of Toronto press, 1963-1991.

----------. "The Spirit of the Age" [Six Parts and first Published in 1831]. In volume XXII of *The Collected Works of John Stuart Mill* (33 Volumes). General Ed. John M. Robson. Toronto: University of Toronto press, 1963-1991, 227-316 *passim*.

----------. *System of Logic* [First published in 1843]. In volumes VII-VIII of *The Collected Works of John Stuart Mill* (33 Volumes). General Ed. John M. Robson. Toronto: University of Toronto press, 1963-1991.

---------. *The Subjection of Women* [First published in 1869]. In volume XXI of *The Collected Works of John Stuart Mill* (33 Volumes). General Ed. John M. Robson. Toronto: University of Toronto press, 1963-1991, 259-340.

----------. *Utilitarianism*. [First published in 1861]. In volume XXI of *The Collected Works of John Stuart Mill* (33 Volumes). General Ed. John M. Robson. Toronto: University of Toronto press, 1963-1991, 203-259.

Mehta, Uday. "Liberal Strategies of Exclusion." *Politics and Society* 18 (1990): 427-454

----------. *Liberalism and Empire: A Study in Nineteenth-Century British Liberal Thought.* London: University of Chicago press, 1999.

Mehta, Pratap. "Liberalism, Nation, and Empire: The Case of J.S. Mill." Paper Presented at the American Political Science Association, San Francisco, 1996.

Morefield, Jeanne. *Covenants Without Swords.* Oxford: Princeton University Press, 2005.

Moirs, Peers, and Zastoupil. Eds. *J.S. Mill's Encounter with India.* Toronto: University of Toronto Press, 1999.

Mommsen. Wolfgang J. *Theories of Imperialism.* London: Weidenfeld and Nicoloson and Random House, 1981

Mantena, Karuna. "Mill and the Imperial Predicament." In *J.S. Mill's Political Thought: A Bicentennial Reassessment.* Eds. Urbinati, Nadia and Alex Zakaras Cambridge: Cambridge University Press, 2007, 298-318.

Morgenbesser, Sidney. "Imperialism: Some Preliminary Distinctions." *Philosophy of Public Affairs* 3:1 (Autumn 1973): 3-44.

Oman, Natalie. "A Critical Assessment of the Responsibility to Prevent". Unpublished manuscript, 2007.

Pankhurst, Richard. *The Saint Simonians, Mill, and Carlyle: a preface to modern thought.* Norwood, Pa: Norwood Editions, 1976.

Parekh, Bhikhu. "Decolonizing Liberalism". *The End of "Isms"?* Ed. Alexandras Shtromas. Oxford: Blackwell, 1994, pp 105-126.

----------. "Liberalism and colonialism: a critique of Locke and Mill." *The Decolonization of Imagination: Culture, Knowledge and Power.* Eds. Jan Nederveen and Bhikhu Parekh. London: Zen books Ltd., 1995, pp 81-98.

----------. "Superior Peoples: The Narrowness of liberalism from Mill to Rawls." *Times Literary Supplement* (February 1994): 11-13.

Passavant, Paul A. and Jodi Dean, eds. *Empire's New Clothes: Reading Hardt and Negri.* New York: Taylor and Francis Books, 2004.

Pitts, Jennifer. *A Turn to Empire: The Rise of Imperial Liberalism in Britain and France.* Oxford: Princeton University Press, 2005.

----------. "James and John Stuart Mill: The Development of Imperial Liberalism in Britain." Chapter Five in Pitts' *A Turn to Empire: The Rise of Imperial Liberalism in Britain and France*. Oxford: Princeton University Press, 2005, 123-162.

Prager, Carol. "Intervention and Empire: John Stuart Mill and International Relations." *Political Studies* 53 (October 2005): 621-640.

Robson, John M. and Michael Laine, eds. *James and John Stuart Mill: Papers of the Centenary Conference*. Toronto: University of Toronto Press, 1976.

Robson, John M. "Civilization and culture as moral concepts." In *The Cambridge Companion to Mill*. Ed. John Skorupski. Cambridge: Cambridge University Press, 1998, 338-371.

----------. *The Improvement of Mankind: The Social and Political Thought of John Stuart Mill*: Toronto: University of Toronto Press, 1968.

Ryan, Alan. *J.S Mill*. London: Routledge & Kegan Paul, 1974.

----------. Bureaucracy, Democracy, Liberty: Some Unanswered Questions in Mill's Politics." In *J.S. Mill's Political Thought: A Bicentennial Reassessment*. Eds. Urbinati, Nadia and Alex Zakaras Cambridge: Cambridge University Press, 2007, 147-165.

----------. "Mill in a Liberal Landscape." In *The Cambridge Companion to Mill*. Ed. John Skorupski. Cambridge: Cambridge University Press, 1998, 497-540.

Said, Edward. *Culture and Imperialism*. New York: Alfred and Knopp, 1993.

Semmel, Bernard. *The rise of free trade imperialism; classical political economy, the empire of free trade and imperialism 1750-1850*. Cambridge: University Press, 1970.

----------. *John Stuart Mill and the Pursuit of Virtue*. New Haven: Yale University Press, 1984.

----------. *The Governor Eyre Controversy*. London: Macgibbon and Kee, 1962.

Skorupski, John ed. *The Cambridge Companion to Mill*. Cambridge, Cambridge: Cambridge University Press, 1998.

Souffrant, Eddy. *Formal Transgression: John Stuart Mill's Philosophy of International Affairs*. Maryland: Rowman and Littlefield Publishers Inc., 2000.

Stanford Encyclopedia of Philosophy. " John Stuart Mill". First published in January
2002 with substantive revision on July, 2006.
http://plato.stanford.edu/entries/mill/ (April 5, 2007).

Sousa Santos, Boaventura de. "Beyond Abyssal Thinking: From Global Lines to
Ecologies of Knowledges." Forthcoming in *Review* (The Journal of the Fernand
Braudel Center SUNY-Binghamton).

----------. "A Critique of Lazy Reason: Against the Waste of Experience." *Eurozine* (
2007): 1-35. Available on the world wide web at the world wide web
http://eurozine.com/pdf/2007-06-29-santos-en.pdf (July 15, 2007).

----------. Ed. *Democratizing Democracy: Beyond the Liberal Democratic Canon*.
London: Verso, 2005.

Sullivan Eileen. "Liberalism and Imperialism: J.S. Mill's Defence of the British Empire."
Journal of the History of Ideas 44:4 (1983): 599-617.

Thomas, William. *Mill*. Oxford: Oxford University Press, 1985.

Tilly, Charles. *Democracy*. Cambridge: Cambridge University Press, 2007.

Tocqueville, Alexis de. *Democracy in America and Two Essays on America*. London:
Penguin Books, 2003.

----------. *Writings on Empire and Slavery*. Edited and Translated by Jennifer Pitts.
Baltimore: Johns Hopkins University Press, 2001.

----------. *Democracy in America: and Two Essays on America*. New York: Penguin,
2003.

Tully, James. *An Approach to Political Philosophy: Locke in Contexts*. Cambridge:
Cambridge University Press, 1993.

----------. "The Imperialism of Modern Constitutionalism.." In *The Paradox of
Constitutionalism: Constituent Power and Consitutional Form*, Eds. Martin
Loughlin and Neil Walker. Oxford: Oxford University Press, 2007, 315-338.

----------. "On Law, Democracy and Imperialism." 21st Annual Public Lecture on Law
and Society, Faculty of Law, 2005. University of Edinburgh, Edinburgh,
Scotland, March 10-11, 2005. Available on the world wide web at
http://web.uvic.ca/polisci/tully/publications/Tully%20Presem%20-
%20Edinburgh%20draft%20criculation%20paper.pdf (July 15, 2007), 1-48.

----------. "The Nature of the 'New' Imperialism." Lecture govern at the Victoria Colloquium & Demcon Conference, University of Victoria, September 30, 2005. Available on the World wide at http://web.uvic.ca/polisci/tully/publications/Nature%20of%20the%20New%20Imperialism%2030%209%202005.pdf (July, 15, 2007), 1-9.

----------. *Strange Multiplicity: Constitutionalism in an age of diversity*. Cambridge: Cambridge University Press, 1995

Tunick, Mark. "Tolerant Imperialism: John Stuart Mill's Defense of British Rule in India." *The Review of Politics* 68 (2006): 586-611

United States. 2006. *National Security Strategy of the United States*. http://www.whitehouse.gov/nsc/nss/2006/ (October 10, 2006).

----------.2002. *National Security Strategy of the United States*. http://www.whitehouse.gov/nsc/nss.html (October 10, 2006).

Urbinati, Nadia and Alex Zakaras. *J.S. Mill's Politcal Thought: A Bicentennial Reassessment*. Cambridge: Cambridge University Press, 2007.

Urbinati, Nadia. .*Mill on democracy: from the Athenian polis to representative government*. Chicago: University of Chicago Press, 2002

----------. *Representative Democracy: Principles and Genealogy*. Chicago: University of Chicago Press, 2006.

----------. "The Many Heads of the Hydra." In *J.S. Mill's Political Thought: A Bicentennial Reassessment*. Eds. Urbinati, Nadia and Alex Zakaras Cambridge: Cambridge University Press, 2007, 66-97.

Varouxakis, Georgios. "Empire, Race, Euro-centrism: John Stuart Mill and His Critics." In *Utilitarianism and Empire*. Edited by Bart Shultz and Georgios Varouxakis. Lanham, MD: Lexington Books, 2005.

Young, Robert. *Postcolonialism: An Historical Introduction*. MA: Blackwell, 2006.

Zakaria, Fareed. *The Future of Freedom: Illiberal Democracy at Home and Abroad*. New York: W.W. Norton and Company, 2003.

Zachary, Karabell. *Parting the Desert: The Creation of the Suez Canal*. New York: Alfred & Knopf, 2003.

Zastoupil, Lynn. *John Stuart Mill and India*. California: Stanford University Press, 1994.

Waltzer, Michael. "Mill's 'A Few Words on Non-Intervention': A Commentary." In *J.S. Mill's Political Thought: A Bicentennial Reassessment*. Eds. Urbinati, Nadia and Alex Zakaras Cambridge: Cambridge University Press, 2007, 347-356.

Weaver, John. *The Great Land Rush and the Making of the Modern World: 1650-1900*. Montreal: McGill-Queen's University Press, 2003.

West, Henry Ed. *The Blackwell Guide to Mill's Utilitarianism*. MA: Blackwell Publishing, 2006.

White, Melanie. "The liberal character of ethological governance." *Economy and Society*. 34 (August 2005): 474-494.

Wilson, Fred. *Psychological Analysis and the Philosophy of John Stuart Mill*. Toronto: University of Toronto Press, 1990.

Wissenschaftlicher Buchverlag bietet

kostenfreie

Publikation

von

wissenschaftlichen Arbeiten

Diplomarbeiten, Magisterarbeiten, Master und Bachelor Theses
sowie Dissertationen, Habilitationen und wissenschaftliche Monographien

Sie verfügen über eine wissenschaftliche Abschlußarbeit zu aktuellen oder zeitlosen
Fragestellungen, die hohen inhaltlichen und formalen Ansprüchen genügt,
und haben **Interesse an einer honorarvergüteten Publikation?**

Dann senden Sie bitte erste Informationen über Ihre Arbeit per Email
an info@vdm-verlag.de. Unser Außenlektorat meldet sich umgehend bei Ihnen.

VDM Verlag Dr. Müller Aktiengesellschaft & Co. KG
Dudweiler Landstraße 125a
D - 66123 Saarbrücken

www.vdm-verlag.de